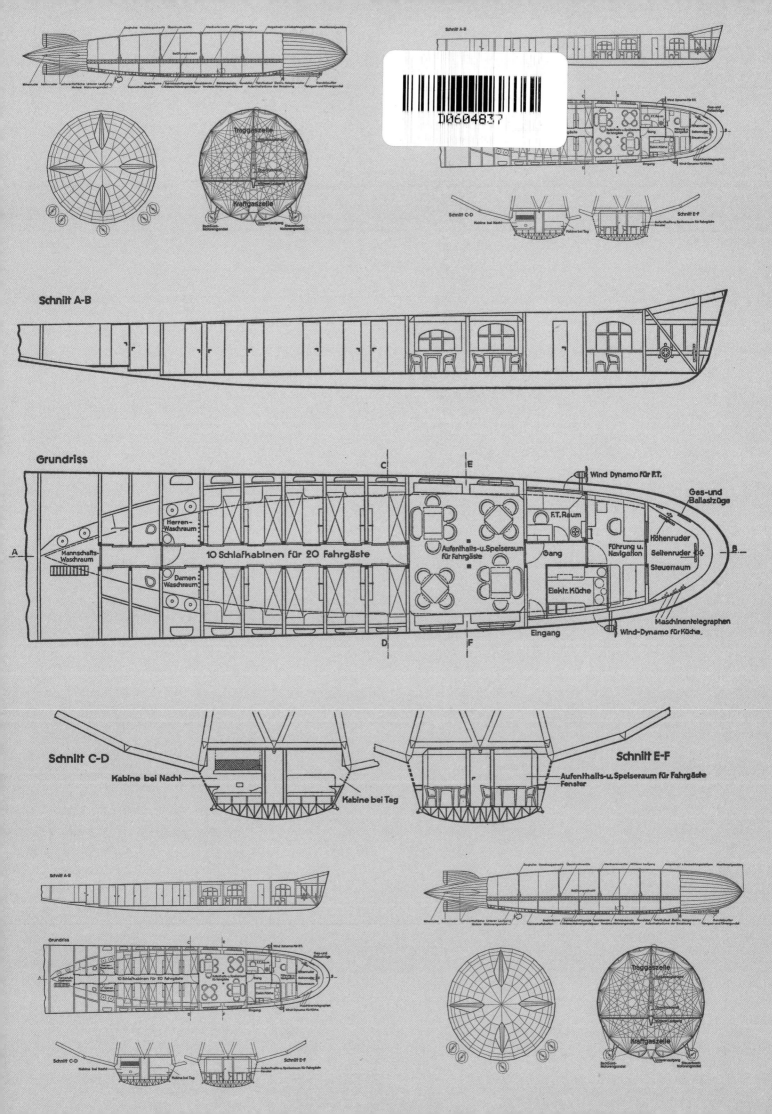

Schnitt A-B

Schnitt A-B

Grundriss

Wind Dynamo für F.T.

Gas-und Ballaszüge

Herren-Waschraum

Höhenruder

Mannschafts-Waschraum

F.T. Raum

10 Schlafkabinen für 20 Fahrgäste

Aufenthalts-u. Speiseraum für Fahrgäste

Führung u. Navigation

Seitenruder

Gang

Damen Waschraum

Elektr. Küche

Steuerraum

Maschinentelegraphen

Eingang

Wind-Dynamo für Küche.

Schnitt C-D

Schnitt E-F

Kabine bei Nacht

Aufenthalts-u. Speiseraum für Fahrgäste Fenster

Kabine bei Tag

Traggaszelle

Kraftgaszelle

# THE ZEPPELIN

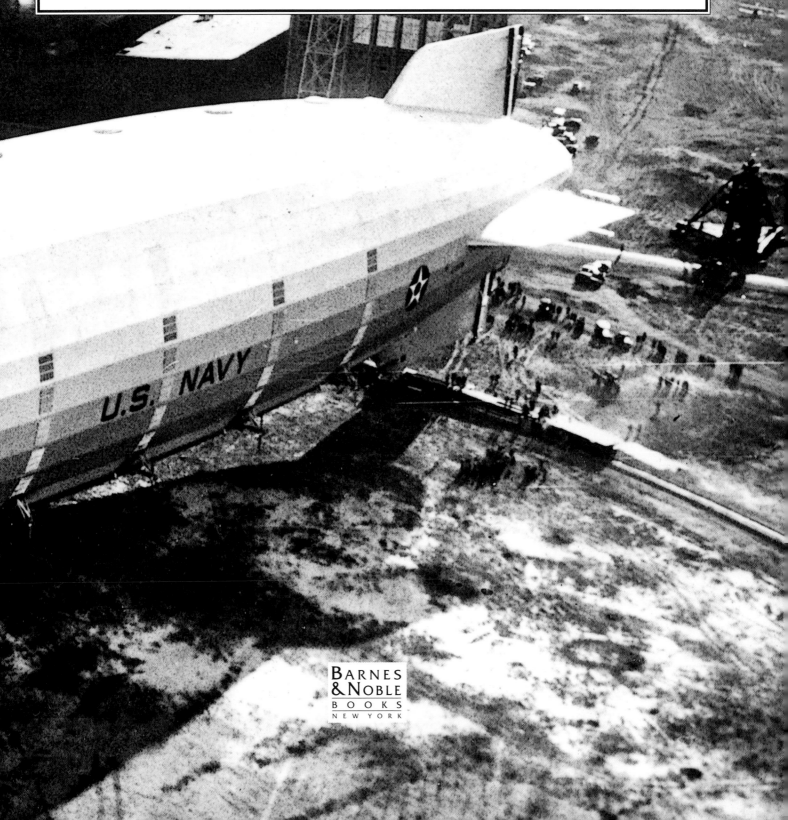

# THE ZEPPELIN

## THE HISTORY OF GERMAN AIRSHIPS FROM 1900 TO 1937

### CHRISTOPHER CHANT

BARNES
&NOBLE
BOOKS
NEW YORK

This edition published by Barnes & Noble, Inc.,
by arrangement with Amber Books Ltd
2000 Barnes & Noble Books

M 10 9 8 7 6 5 4 3 2 1

ISBN: 0-7607-1996-9

Editorial and design by
Amber Books Ltd
Bradley's Close
74-77 White Lion Street
London N1 9PF

Project Editor: Antonia Maxwell
Design: Zoë Mellors
Picture Research: Lisa Wren

Printed in Italy

**Picture credits**

All photographic material supplied by TRH Pictures,
except page 76, supplied by Popperfoto.

# Contents

*Originally operated from a floating hangar that could be turned into alignment with the wind, the Zeppelin airship was a truly remarkable achievement. The complex tail surface arrangement on the LZ3 (1906) was typical of the early Zeppelin airships.*

# Designers of the Zeppelin

The dream of flight is perhaps as old as man himself, and there can be few who have never dreamed of flight in one way or another, taking to the air like a soaring bird or a floating cloud. In ancient times, the dream spawned legends such as that of Daedalus and Icarus, and from medieval and renaissance times there were the first tentative attempts to create a reality out of the dreams with at least semi-realistic plans for flying machines.

The efforts of men such as Leonardo da Vinci in the late fourteenth and early fifteenth centuries were all stymied by an apparently intractable trio of circumstances: the lack of a true scientific basis from which to undertake their developments, the absence of materials that were both strong and light, and the non-availability of any power source other than a man's musculature. Creeping progress was nonetheless made over the following centuries, and in 1783 man first took to the air in a hot-air balloon. The science and art of ballooning developed steadily if intermittently, and once man had mastered the ability to rise into the air and descend safely, it was inevitable that he should try to devise a means of moving through the air in a purposeful manner, rather than merely floating at the whim of the air currents.

There was considerable progress in the evolution of the required type of dirigible balloon, or airship, in the later part of the nineteenth century as a more or less effective means of propulsion became available. The man who finally turned the dream into reality, in terms of creating a fully controlled airship capable of carrying a worthwhile payload in safety, was a retired German army officer, Ferdinand von Zeppelin, whose name became and in fact largely remains synonymous with lighter-than-air travel.

### ZEPPELIN FAMILY HISTORY

In the medieval period there appeared in the low, flat lands bordering the coast of the Baltic Sea in north Germany a large number of Slav immigrants, the Wendes, who found the region suitable for settlement. The most distinctive element of the region's fauna was the czapla, or stork, which bred in large numbers, and after which the Wendes named the region. Over the years the name was slowly transmuted to Cepelin, Sepelin, Zepelyn, and eventually Zepelin. The first settlement named Zepelin, in Mecklenburg, is first recorded in 1246, and the first person with this name is first chronicled in 1286. The family of this man held the land for more than 500 years, and distinguished themselves largely as soldiers and, in later times, as diplomats in the services of the various dukes of Württemberg and, to a lesser extent, other rulers in Austro-Hungary, Denmark and Russia.

In 1834, the Graf Friedrich von Zeppelin, as the family now spelled its name to reflect the softer speech of southern Germany, moved to an estate at Konstanz near the body of water known as the Bodensee (Lake Constance). He married Amelie Macaire d'Hogguer from a wealthy French family who had moved from Geneva, and the pair had three children, namely their daughter Eugenie born in 1836, their first son Ferdinand born in 1838, and their second son Eberhard born in 1842.

The first son, and therefore heir to the von Zeppelin title and estates, was in fact Ferdinand Adolf August Heinrich von Zeppelin. He was born on 8 July 1838 at the home of his grandparents on an island in Lake Constance. Ferdinand's mother had herself been born 22 years earlier on this same island, which was sited at the point where the Rhine leaves Lake Constance, adjacent to the town of Konstanz. Two years after Ferdinand's birth the family bought an estate at Girsberg from the Duke of Württemberg and moved to this less damp abode.

### EDUCATING THE YOUNG FERDINAND VON ZEPPELIN

The count and countess were retiring people, not at all like the stereotypical German nobility with their overbearing manner and relatively little education. Indeed, the countess in particular was adamant that her children were not to be brought up with an air of natural superiority. They were educated at home in what was for the time a very liberal fashion, and considerable emphasis was placed on their health through adequate exercise and no overindulgence in food. Most of the time the children played outside, and became keen walkers and swimmers. Although they were knowledgeable about the flora and fauna of southern Germany, they led sheltered lives, and their first real experience of life outside the family estate began in 1848, when the family home needed extensive repairs: Amelie and the three children stayed temporarily at Castell, a small village just outside Konstanz, while the count stayed with the grandparents at Konstanz, where the children would visit him.

During this period, the revolutionary unrest gripping many parts of Europe also touched Württemberg, and the young Ferdinand von Zeppelin was fascinated by the whole process, which he saw in the drilling of the insurgent forces in the streets and the many speeches made by local leaders pronouncing revolutionary activity. Most of the leaders had turned to Württemberg after the failure of their efforts in Prussia, the largest and most powerful of the German states, and in the circumstances is was hardly surprising that Prussia, under the leadership of King (later Emperor) Friedrich Wilhelm, was the main force in the final crushing of revolutionary efforts in Germany.

With the repairs at Girsberg completed, the von Zeppelin family returned to their home, which in a consciously anachronistic fashion they preferred to call Obergyrsberg. The children embarked on a secondary education under a different tutor who, despite his primary predilection for ancient languages and theology, was largely successful in imparting a general sense of enthusiasm and interest into the children, whose education was

LEFT *Ferdinand, Graf von Zeppelin was a remarkable man, who became devoted to the concept of the lighter-than-air ship only at the end of a long and moderately successful army career.*

thereby expanded to included subjects such as geography and history, all within the context of a programme that emphasised an enquiring attitude of mind rather than learning by rote.

Soon after the children had completed three years of their education under the supervision of another tutor, Robert Moser, the delicate health of their mother took a turn for the worse. Amelie von Zeppelin moved to a sanatorium at Montpellier in France, and died there in 1852. The death of their beloved mother was a severe blow to the children, and the count had to put his foot down to prevent Ferdinand from pursuing a resultant determination to become a missionary. Instead, during 1853 the young Ferdinand was enrolled in a secondary school (the Gymnasium) at Stuttgart, where he entered the top class. The emphasis here was on the sciences, most particularly physics, chemistry and mathematics. Ferdinand von Zeppelin graduated from the Gymnasium in October 1854 and then entered the Kriegsschule, or military academy, at Ludwigsburg, just a short distance to the north of Stuttgart.

ABOVE *The pioneering LZ1 is seen here in 1900 in the floating erection shed and hangar at Manzell on Lake Constance.*

BELOW *The LZ1 on its maiden flight, 2 July 1900. The size of the airship is indicated by the diminutive scale of the men on the floating platform beneath.*

## AN ARMY CAREER

Graduating from the Kriegsschule in March 1857 at the age of 20, Ferdinand von Zeppelin began an army career as a lieutenant in the 8th Württemberg Infantry Regiment, although in the short term he was attached to the quartermaster corps of the general staff. The young officer was as little at home with the conventional regimentation and discipline of the army life as he had been with the similar conditions prevalent in the Kriegsschule; such conditions did not sit well on the shoulders of a young man who was naturally an individual and who had enjoyed in his youth an education that reinforced this tendency. In an effort to broaden his horizons still further, he planned to enrol at the celebrated University of Tübingen. He had been in the army at Württemberg for about one year, when he asked the war office for a leave of absence, which was readily granted. The young nobleman travelled forthwith to Tübingen, where he studied chemistry, engineering and politics.

It was during this period that the Emperor Napoleon III demanded the cession to France of the regions of Savoy and Nice, and from the beginning of 1859 France, allied secretly with Piedmont (the Kingdom of Sardinia) started to exert pressure on the Austro-Hungarian Empire. After Piedmont had mobilised in March 1859, Austro-Hungary had little choice but to follow suit in the following month and demand an immediate Piedmontese demobilisation. This triggered overt intervention by France on the side of Piedmont, and Austro-Hungary felt, despite the uncertainty of Prussian and other German aid, that military operations were required and launched a somewhat

ABOVE *The LZ2 of 1905 reflected the lessons learned with the LZ1 and was a much neater airship. A salient feature was the basically cylindrical hull with tapered bow and stern sections.*

half-hearted invasion of Piedmont. There was a large-scale mobilisation of the various armies of the federal German state that had been established in February 1849 by the Frankfurt constitution under Kaiser Friedrich Wilhelm.

Ferdinand von Zeppelin left Tübingen to join the corps of engineers stationed at Ulm. For a member of the German nobility to join the engineer corps, which was deemed an artisan force to be officered by members of the middle class, was unusual and Ferdinand von Zeppelin received a large measure of disapproval from family and friends. However, it was an action increasingly typical of this young man and his individualistic nature.

As a result of the very poor leadership of General Franz Graf von Gyulai, the Austro-Hungarian forces soon lost the strategic initiative and were beaten in several battles by the smaller forces of the Piedmontese and later French armies. Neither side wanted Germany, under Prussian leadership, to enter the war, and peace negotiations were quickly begun in July, and as a result the recently mobilised regiment at Ulm never got into action at all. Ferdinand von Zeppelin's superior officers were pleased with the spirit of aggression and the efficiency he had displayed at this time, however, and in 1862, just before the signature of the peace agreement that yielded most of Lombardy to Piedmont, the young officer was promoted to first lieutenant and transferred back to the general staff.

## BROADENING HORIZONS

When, at the start of 1863, the orders for junior officers of the Württemberg army's general staff were issued, the young Ferdinand von Zeppelin was unhappy with the severe lack of imagination they revealed, for he felt that the very nature of the German type of professional military organisation needed to be explored more fully, especially in regard to its capability vis-à-vis the type of militia organisation favoured in countries such as the USA to provide a war-time numerical boost to very small professional cadre forces. Ferdinand von Zeppelin felt that professionalism offered the way forward, but wanted to assess the reality of the situation for himself and therefore requested assignment as a military observer in the American Civil War (1861–65). The young officer's father was strongly opposed to this idea, but was then gradually won round to his son's thinking, although still with strong reservations about the dangers of the concept and the unlikelihood, as the elder von Zeppelin believed, of an

LEFT *Tethered balloons, of the type seen here in the American Civil War, were the first practical hydrogen-filled 'aircraft' to be used for short-range reconnaissance of the enemy's front-line dispositions and defences.*

BELOW *This photograph of the crashed LZ2 reveals its structure, with gas cells inside a light alloy framework covered with fabric to reduce the drag generated in forward flight.*

LEFT *The sight of the early Zeppelin airships in flight (here the LZ3) was monumentally impressive, and helped to convince all that man was really becoming master of the air.*

RIGHT *The Graf von Zeppelin and his daughter in the control gondola of the LZ3. Little concession was made to comfort in the design of the early gondolas.*

observer really being allowed to see anything of value. In order to secure high-ranking support for his request for leave to travel to the USA, Ferdinand von Zeppelin approached his cousin, the Baron von Maucler, who was cabinet chief of Kaiser Friedrich Wilhelm. In a letter to his cousin, he wrote:

> *I believe it is my duty to use this opportunity through travel to gain information that I may be able to use for my fatherland at some time. Despite a totally chaotic situation, North America still offers the richest rewards at the present. The investigative observer can find the solution to problems that also will be of value to us, in the organisation, leadership and supply of the armies there, particularly since these are being administered under distinctly unfavourable and quite unusual conditions. The Americans are especially inventive in the adaptation of technical developments for military purposes. I do not need to mention the benefits which such a journey promises to have for the general enlightenment.*

However, even before von Maucler received this letter, the 24-year-old Ferdinand von Zeppelin had been given a year's leave. His desire to reach the USA as soon as possible was evident in his refusal to act as best man at a close friend's wedding. Travelling by way of London, where he spent a short time, Ferdinand departed Liverpool in April 1863 on a Cunard steamship and arrived in New York in the early part of May. Even after his arrival in the USA, the young German officer did not waste time as he was anxious to see the war as soon as possible. After a short visit to Philadelphia, he travelled to Baltimore on a French warship with documents written in French, the language generally used for international documentation at the time, designating him as the Comte Zeppelin, Chargé d'affaires de Son Majesté le Roi de Württemberg.

Reaching Baltimore, Ferdinand von Zeppelin then travelled overland to Washington, DC, where he found the drab and dusty atmosphere a severe disappointment, even though the presence of many men in uniform (many of them Europeans seeking appointments in the Federal army) indicated that this was a city currently devoted to war rather than civilian matters. In Washington, von Zeppelin presented himself to the German official, the Hanseatic ambassador, Doktor Rudolf von Schleiden, to whom he carried a letter of introduction. Von Schleiden introduced von Zeppelin to the Prussian ambassador, who was able to arrange an interview with President Abraham Lincoln. Before this, the president had written to Secretary of State, William H. Seward, and Secretary of War, Edwin M. Stanton, asking if the German officer should be given a military pass. All three senior members of the administration being in agreement, von Zeppelin received a pass signed by the president and giving the bearer complete freedom of movement within the areas controlled by the Federal armies.

Von Zeppelin then had a meeting with Lieutenant General Daniel Butterfield, chief-of-staff of the Army of the Potomac, who advised the German officer on how best to get to the army in the field on the front not far to the south of Washington. Keen to reach the front as soon as possible, von Zeppelin bought the necessary equipment and had a tailor make him a uniform, which differed from the regulation Württemberg model quite considerably, but was well adapted to the climate and geography of the USA's eastern seaboard. Von Zeppelin later noted that his lieutenant's star insignia were very similar to that of a Federal Brigadier general, and he was often mistaken for such an exalted officer. Von Zeppelin also secured the use of a horse from a former Prussian cavalry guard officer, Colonel von Radowitz, who was now an officer of the Federal army, to which he was the primary supplier of horses. For his horse, von Zeppelin did not opt for an English saddle but for a wooden saddle of the type used by the US Army. He found this a truly excellent item of equipment, even though it was somewhat different from the saddle to which he was accustomed. Von

Zeppelin brought this saddle back to Germany at the end of his time in the USA. To complete his 'team' for the field, von Zeppelin secured the services of a Negro groom and a cook.

### THE ARMY OF THE POTOMAC

To reach the Army of the Potomac, von Zeppelin travelled down the Potomac river from Washington by steamer and then headed south towards Falmouth, Virginia, by narrow-gauge railway from Aquia Creek. The headquarters of the Army of the Potomac was a sizeable camp in a region of thin woods, and on the day that he reached the army von Zeppelin had his first real encounter with modern warfare as, towards the evening, he rode with a Russian officer to see what was happening after artillery fire had been heard from the direction of the Rappahannock river. The two men soon found themselves amid exploding shells, and von Zeppelin suggested that it might be sensible to ride off to the side away from the area being shelled, and thus to observe the action rather than become embroiled in it. He later offered the opinion that he felt it required more courage to move out of the danger area than it would have required to stay within it.

The shelling stopped, and as they rode back towards the headquarters of the Army of the Potomac, the Russian officer asked von Zeppelin to ride on alone as he had other business requiring his attention. Von Zeppelin, suspecting that this was some kind of espionage, agreed and set off on his own along the edge of a forest. He later encountered a piquet line at which he was able to find the direction of headquarters. On the way the German officer met no other living creature, until he was finally challenged by a sentry, to whom he was able to respond with the right password.

When General Joseph Hooker, commanding the Army of the Potomac, returned to his command some days later after a visit to Washington, von Zeppelin presented his presidential pass and was able to start work on his observation of the Federal army. Von Zeppelin accompanied the formations and units of the Army of the Potomac whenever and wherever possible, and on one occasion had a lucky escape. Attached to Major General Alfred Pleasonton's cavalry formation, von Zeppelin requested and received permission to accompany a cavalry operation designed to secure useful information on the Confederate dispositions in the Shenandoah valley after pushing aside the cavalry screen found by the troops of Major General J.E.B. Stuart, one of the finest cavalry commanders of the war. The Federal force rapidly made contact with the Confederate screen, and each group of cavalry then advanced with covering fire provided by its own side's artillery. The regiments of each side then accelerated their trot to a canter, and finally a gallop, as they approached their opposite numbers to attack with carbine and sabre before pulling back to regroup and then attack once more.

Gradually the Federal cavalry began to gain the upper hand, and at this stage the Confederate cavalry pulled back behind a small river, where the waiting Confederate infantry and artillery gave the advancing Federal cavalry a hot reception. By this time von Zeppelin, riding on the right wing of the Federal advance, had become involved in the attack and inadvertently penetrated the Confederate line. Luckily for the future of airship development, the German officer was able to extricate himself and set off back towards the main body of the Federal force, benefiting from the greater speed of his horse to escape from a party of pursuing Confederates mounted on average army horses. It is possible that von Zeppelin would have been killed had the Confederate riders caught him, but to reduce the chances of ill-treatment or even summary execution, von Zeppelin carried in the lining of his coat a personal letter of introduction to General Robert E. Lee, the Confederate commander, from his niece, whom von Zeppelin had met in Philadelphia.

BELOW *The LZ4 of 1908 is seen here low over the water against a backdrop of sightseeing boats, which were useful for rescue purposes on occasion.*

ABOVE *The wreckage of the LZ4, lost to fire in 1908. Such a loss was always a grisly sight, and generally resulted in a high casualty rate if the fire occurred in flight.*

### JOURNEY ACROSS AMERICA

In the event, von Zeppelin probably left the Army of the Potomac towards the end of June 1863, when Hooker was relieved of his command. He returned to New York in time to witness the great riots that took place between 13 and 15 July of the same year in protest at the Conscription Act passed by Congress in March 1863. The riots were notably bitter in Boston and New York, and ended only after about 1,000 people had been killed. Von Zeppelin remained in New York for only a couple of days, before setting off by train for the west.

From New York, von Zeppelin travelled to Ohio and thence by steamship over the Great Lakes to Michigan and by portage route to Minnesota, where he travelled along the line of the Mississippi from Crow Wing to St Cloud by stagecoach and finally by hired coach to St Paul. It was here that there was a turning point in von Zeppelin's life, for it was outside this city that the German officer saw and then ascended in a balloon designed and operated by John H. Steiner, who had been a member of the balloon corps attached to the Federal army under the command of Thaddeus S.C. Lowe. Von Zeppelin found the balloon fascinating on two counts: the opportunities it provided to him as a military officer to gain first-hand experience of the balloon's capabilities for tactical reconnaissance and, as a man of scientific leaning, to rise well above the ground for the first time in a device of man's own invention.

St Paul was as far to the west as von Zeppelin reached in the USA, and from Minnesota the German officer returned to New York where, in November 1863, he boarded ship for his return to Europe, where the temperature of international relations was running hot, although there was to be no war for another three years.

### WAR AT HOME

Von Zeppelin was 26 years old when he returned from his American adventure to the humdrum existence of a junior officer in the army of Württemberg. Then, in 1866, war broke out between Prussia and Austro-Hungary as a result of the latter's fears about the nature and extent of Prussia's increasing involvement in the power politics of central Europe, as evidenced by the Prussian occupation of Holstein and its signature of a secret treaty with France. The extent of Prussia's growth of power in the region was also troubling a number of German states, and as a result several of them, including Württemberg, allied themselves with Austro-Hungary.

By this time von Zeppelin had been promoted to Captain and appointed as the personal adjutant to the King of Württemberg. Despite the semi-court nature of his appointment, von Zeppelin did see some service during the seven-week war, first on the very edges of the small battles of Tauberbischofsheim and Würzburg, and later played a slight part in the action of the somewhat larger battle of

BELOW *The Graf von Zeppelin and Hugo Eckener, who became increasingly important in the Zeppelin organisation, in the control gondola of the Schwaben, probably in 1912.*

Aschaffenburg. The involvement of the Württemberg army was on the periphery of the main campaign, which the Prussians won at Königgrätz in July 1866. After this the parties were brought together by French mediation and the war was settled in Prussia's favour by the Treaty of Prague, in which Austro-Hungary forewent any right to become involved in German affairs. The German states north of the Main river were formed into a North German Confederation under Prussian leadership, and the German states south of the river were allowed to create an independent confederation.

Shortly after the conclusion of hostilities, Kronprinz Wilhelm of Württemberg was posted to Potsdam, the Prussian capital, as an officer in the Prussian Guard, and von Zeppelin received an appointment as the prince's personal adjutant. In was during this period that von Zeppelin decided to marry, his intended wife being the Freiin Isabella von Wolff, a lady from the long-established German-Latvian family of Alt Schwanenberg. The couple were married in July 1869, and had a daughter, Helene, in 1879.

Before the marriage took place, however, von Zeppelin had become bored with the routine of everyday military life, which was in fact more social than military for the better-born officers, and decided to broaden his horizons. In 1868 von Zeppelin

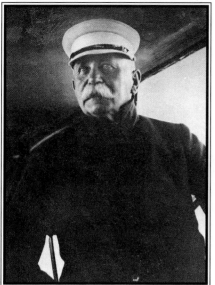

ABOVE *The Graf von Zeppelin, the founder and driving force behind the Zeppelin airship.*

ABOVE *Hugo Eckener saw the Zeppelin organisation as the basis of a world-girdling transport company.*

ABOVE *Ludwig Dürr, chief engineer, led the design and construction of the Zeppelin airships up to the end of World War I.*

therefore requested and was granted a transfer to the intelligence department of the army. In this capacity, von Zeppelin travelled through much of eastern France to assess and report on the nature of the French defences, most notably the fortifications, as relations between Prussia and France were deteriorating rapidly and the power of Germany, under the political leadership of Chancellor Otto von Bismarck, continued to grow.

The final spur to the Franco-Prussian War that broke out in July 1870, was the threat that the Emperor Napoleon III perceived in von Bismarck's attempt to place a prince of the Prussian royal house on the throne of Spain, which would have caught France in a grand strategic vice. The emperor, wrongly believing that the French army was superior to that of the Germans in every respect, actively precipitated the war against a generally united Germany that was, in fact, far better prepared for war than France. By this time von Zeppelin was attached to the general staff of the Württemberg cavalry, which formed part of the III Corps under the command of the crown prince of Prussia.

In the mobile phase of the war, which lasted only two months before the German forces invested the French capital, Paris, von Zeppelin saw only limited action in a border skirmish as he was undertaking a reconnaissance with a small party of cavalry. During the siege of Paris, however, von Zeppelin renewed his acquaintance with the balloon, which the French used cleverly to send messages and to transport 164 persons out of the invested city whenever the wind was blowing in the right direction to carry their free balloons over the Germans' heads towards the part of France unoccupied by the Germans.

The Franco-Prussian War ended in February 1871 with the capitulation of France, which lost the regions of Alsace and Lorraine to Germany and had to pay a sizeable indemnity. Just as importantly, even as the siege of Paris was continuing, the culmination of von Bismarck's long-term manoeuvring was reached on 18 January 1871 with the proclamation of a united German empire under Wilhelm of Prussia, who thus became Emperor of Germany.

### An Idea is Born

Returning to the type of military life typical of peace time, von Zeppelin was now highly enthused about the possibilities of the balloon, whose main limitation he saw as its necessary subjection to the vagaries of the wind after it had been released, as indicated by the number of French balloons that had fallen into German hands when the wind had changed after they had been released in Paris. Spurred by a small book on the potential of the steerable balloon for postal purposes, *Weltpost und Luftschiffahrt* published in 1870 by Heinrich von Stephan, the postmaster of the North German Confederation, von Zeppelin began to feel that the future lay with the steerable or dirigible balloon, which would have military as well as civil applications.

Von Zeppelin soon drafted the basic design for a dirigible balloon and, as he himself later said: 'My goal is clear, my calculations are correct.' Oddly enough, von Zeppelin never revealed the nature of these goals or the calculations of his dirigible balloon. In 1874, he was injured in a riding accident and had to remain in the hospital at Strasbourg for some time, where he devoted much of his enforced inactivity to

ABOVE *Encapsulating the period before the outbreak of World War I, this photograph shows the Viktoria Luise airship over the magnificent yachts taking part in the Kiel Regatta of 1912.*

reading and thinking about dirigible balloons. His wife later said that he had first told her about his plans for a rigid airship during this period.

The end of the Franco-Prussian War and the declaration of the German empire, or more formally the Confederation of German States, resulted in a wholesale reorganisation of the German military machine to bring the armies of the smaller states into alignment with that of Prussia. As a result, in 1872 von Zeppelin had been posted to the 15th Schleswig-Holstein Lancer Regiment, which was stationed at Strasbourg. After his emergence from hospital, von Zeppelin was promoted to major, and was now able to arrange for a transfer to his old unit, the 26th Dragoon Regiment stationed at Ulm. Further promotion followed in due course, and in 1882 von Zeppelin was elevated to the rank of Colonel and given command of the 19th Uhlan Regiment based at Stuttgart.

Soon after this, however, von Zeppelin once more became disenchanted with the lassitude of peacetime soldiering and in 1885 was able to use his influence to secure a transfer, in this instance as the military attaché to the Württemberg legation in

Berlin, the German capital to which all the previously independent kingdoms, duchies and free cities of Germany now sent an ambassadorial team: the ambassadors in effect constituted the upper parliamentary house of the new empire, of which von Zeppelin became a member in 1887.

A number of intellectuals and military leaders were wont to gather at the von Zeppelin home on the Vosstrasse, and in this fashion the increasingly air-minded von Zeppelin gradually made the acquaintance of many leading German scientists, including the pre-eminent physicist, anatomist, and physiologist Professor Hermann Ludwig Ferdinand von Helmholtz, the most illustrious of the group of influential scientific heavyweights of the period.

During those years, many trial balloons were launched in several parts of Europe. A US citizen living in France, F.A. Gower, had succeeded in steering his fish-shaped balloon in 1883 across the English Channel, using petroleum in a bronze steam engine to produce 5hp (3.7kW). During a later experiment, Gower was unfortunately drowned in that same English Channel, but his pioneering work had already had a pronounced effect on von Zeppelin.

By 1884 the German army had a regular balloon detachment, and in 1887 the military budget included funding for the support of this group, whose personnel comprised a major, a captain, four lieutenants, and one regular-sized company of enlisted men. Initially the unit had no balloons of its own: a free balloon was leased for the weekly training periods from a female acrobat, Kätchen Paulus, who used it every Sunday when the weather permitted for an ascent at a popular local resort for Berliners. At one time, members of the general staff were invited to attend a demonstration of the parachute by a circus daredevil.

## STEERABILITY AND PROPULSION

Von Zeppelin was more interested in the work of a French pioneer, Colonel Charles Renard, who had built a steerable balloon for his government in 1884. This elongated balloon comprised a large gas envelope filled with lifting gas and regulated by means of ventilators. To the lower portion of this envelope was attached a long wooden frame, which held this relevant part of the envelope quite rigid. At the end of the framework there was a large wooden propeller for propulsion. The idea was workable in its essential form, but unfortunately for Renard his dirigible balloon's electric motor and batteries were too heavy and their power too low to propel the balloon effectively. Other types of power unit, such as combustion engines, were insufficiently developed for practical use at this time, but did offer the promise of lower weight and greater power as they were progressed. By this time, it should be noted, von Zeppelin was a firm believer in the notion that the envelope of the dirigible balloon should be of an elongated rather than a spherical shape, in order to penetrate the air rather than ride at the behest of its currents. He also believed that it should be rigid to ensure that its shape was maintained as a primary necessity for 'steerability'.

In an 1887 report to the King of Württemberg, von Zeppelin pointed out that if the dirigible balloon, or more properly the airship, was ever to be of importance in military matters it would have to be manoeuvrable in the face of powerful air currents. It would also have to be able to remain in the air without landing for at least 24 hours, in order that it could travel a considerable distance from its base to undertake a useful reconnaissance before returning. Furthermore, it would have to be designed and manufactured to carry a sizeable load of men, ammunition, and supplies. It was a corollary of these three basic requirements that a large quantity of lifting gas would have to be provided to support the whole structure, which would necessarily be somewhat massive. In short, the provision of a genuine utility would require the design and construction of a large airship. Von Zeppelin was also adamant that an elongated shape, with a rigid structure, was the only way to ensure that the airship could be steered on its intended course. He was less certain about the specific shape, which would have to be decided empirically after experiments and trials had been carried out. Von Zeppelin felt there were two other aspects that

would have to be investigated so that a practical solution could be achieved. These were how to rise in the air without having to release ballast, which would of course be of finite quantity and limited in overall weight to avoid affecting the airship's performance, and how to descend without venting and thereby wasting lifting gas, which was expensive to manufacture. Von Zeppelin concluded that if it became possible to solve these problems, the significance of the airship would become genuinely considerable, for the type of aerial ship that was anticipated would have uses in both the civil and military spheres.

Von Zeppelin predicted that the airship would be able to provide the shortest journeys across mountains, across the sea, or between any two given points, and could also be used for exploration in areas such as central Africa or the polar regions. This was a very far-sighted report, but there is no proof that it was seen by anyone in authority before being filed away in the archives of the Kingdom of Württemberg.

## BACK IN THE ARMY

While his interest in aeronautical matters continued to increase, von Zeppelin had been elevated to the position of ambassador to Prussia in 1887. However, the related worlds of diplomacy and politics did not really catch his imagination, and in 1889 he was happy to relinquish his diplomatic status to re-embark in January 1890 on his military career as the Brigadier general commanding the 30th Cavalry Brigade based in Saarburg. Soon after the spring manoeuvres of 1890, however, von Zeppelin was placed on the retired list, a matter which considerably surprised him as he had expected to be elevated to the command of a division. This totally unexpected retirement was a major psychological blow to von Zeppelin, who was now 52 and in what he thought was the prime of his career, especially as it was unusual for any commander to be retired immediately after the completion of manoeuvres.

There was considerable speculation within the army about the reasons for the retirement, and it is undeniable that von Zeppelin's strong character had led to disagreements with the high command's orthodox military thinking. It is possible that the retirement came as a result of what the high command believed to be some type of insubordination.

Von Zeppelin and his family now moved into a large house in Stuttgart and, while spending most of the year in the Württemberg capital, they generally spent the summer at their Girsberg estate on the Bodensee. However, what most of his friends and acquaintances must have imagined would become a period of leisure and reflection actually marked the beginning of von Zeppelin's most important work as a devotee of airships. He acquired virtually every book available and had soon learned a great deal.

Von Zeppelin now found he had the time to familiarise himself more fully with aerostatics, the scientific discipline concerned with the balance of gaseous fluids and the equilibrium and buoyancy of bodies immersed in such fluids. Although this discipline applies formally only to gases and bodies that are at rest, its principles are also applicable to some gases and objects in motion. The retired general discovered, for instance, that a body submerged in air actually experiences a measure of buoyancy force that causes the body to rise, and thus that a lighter-than-air craft floats in the air whenever the weight of the gas container and all attached objects, plus the weight of the lifting gas, equals the weight of the displaced air.

By this time von Zeppelin was fully cognisant with the increasingly arcane terminology associated with lighter-than-air craft, and knew that a balloon (fabricated of a light impermeable material filled with heated air or gas lighter than air) is an aerostat without a propulsion system: a captive balloon is one connected to the ground by a cable, while a free balloon is one whose ascent and descent can be controlled by the release of ballast or the venting of the lifting gas. Observation balloons of the type now increasingly common in the world's more advanced armies were usually of the captive type, generally manned so that the desired reconnaissance could be undertaken. While the earliest balloons were merely spherical, the steerable types that were increasingly the object of study and experimentation were notable for their adoption of an elongated shape for improved 'steerability'.

### A BRIEF HISTORY OF THE BALLOON

The origins of the balloon can be traced far back into history. In 1670, for example, the Jesuit Francisco Lana-Teni of Brescia, observing that smoke or other gases lighter than air rose into the sky, reasoned that a vessel from which the air had been removed would also rise and even carry something aloft. He therefore planned a vehicle comprising four copper balls from which all the air had been evacuated, so that the balls thus weighed less than the air they would displace. The concept was theoretically valid, but was never put to the test because of its originator's religious convictions. In fact, the fabrication of copper spheres strong enough not to collapse under the pressure of the outside air would have been wholly impossible, and the structure Lana designed would also have been too heavy to rise from the ground.

Perhaps the first man to demonstrate that a built object could really rise into the air was another Jesuit, Bartholomo Laurenco de Gusmao of Brazil. In about 1720, de Gusmao built a balloon and demonstrated his invention in Portugal before a distinguished audience, which included royalty: the balloon rose to the ceiling of a huge ballroom.

About a quarter of a century later, a pamphlet on the 'Art of Navigation in the Air' was published in Avignon by Father Joseph Gallien who, in order not to jeopardise his future in the Church, said that what was in fact a serious thesis should be seen merely as a 'physical and geometric amusement'. To be able to rise, a vessel would not only have to be airless, but would have to contain air lighter than that found at sea level, perhaps from higher altitudes. Miscalculating badly, Gallien offered the opinion that a vessel with a capacity of $100ft^3$ ($2.8m^3$) would have a lifting power of 7.5 billion lb (3.4 billion kg).

The problem of 'lighter air' was solved in 1766 when an Englishman, Henry Cavendish, discovered hydrogen gas. This was very difficult to manufacture with the technology of the day, however, so early balloonists used hot air instead. In a paper bag factory at Annonay, one of the owners noticed one day that such a bag rose mysteriously into the air: it had been placed over a pot of boiling water and filled with steam. The brothers Joseph Michel and Jacques Etienne Montgolfier became intrigued, and in 1782 constructed a balloon that they placed over an open firepit. The silk envelope filled with smoke and rose. A year later the brothers built a balloon holding $13,430ft^3$ ($380m^3$) of hot air, attached a basket carrying some animals, and sent it into the air, in which it reached an altitude of some 6,000ft (1,830m) and covered a ground distance of 7,668ft (2,337m).

When King Louis XVI was invited to witness an ascent by the two brothers, he forbade them to undertake such a risk. Instead, two condemned criminals were summoned to become the first passengers until public opposition led to a further change of regal mind and two gentlemen, the Marquis d'Arlandes and M. Pilâtre de Rozier, shared the honour of making the world's first human ascent into the air on 21 November 1783.

The record shows that the sky was flecked with cloud, and that there was a slight wind from the northwest. The balloon was filled within eight minutes and was ready to start its journey. At the first launch attempt a slight wind took the balloon which, instead of rising vertically, crabbed up sideways. Despite the efforts of the ground crew holding its tether ropes, the balloon collided with some tall trees. It was returned to the launch platform and once again filled with hot air. Two hours later, at exactly 1.54 p.m., it rose majestically to a height of about 250ft (75m), and the proud passengers raised their hats in greeting to the assembled spectators on the ground. Everyone there felt fear and admiration. The balloon rose to an altitude of at least 3,000ft (915m), and as it floated over the River Seine, all of the citizens of Paris could see it. Satisfied with their test flight, the balloonists decided to land but, as they were over the houses of the city, they climbed again and finally landed in a meadow near the Moulin Croulebarbe. They still had about two-thirds of their supplies and thus could have stayed aloft for a much longer time than the 25 minutes they spent in the air. The balloon's first passenger flight had been a spectacular success.

Elienne Montgolfier

Joseph Montgolfier

ABOVE *The Montgolfier brothers of France have an enduring place in aviation history as the designers and constructors of the first man-made device to lift off the ground and float through the sky.*

Jacques Alexandre César Charles, another Frenchman, was a scientist familiar with the theories of Lana and the discovery of hydrogen gas. He decided to make a balloon filled with hydrogen rather than hot air so that it could lift a greater load and remain in the air longer than the Montgolfiers' balloon. It was only three months after the first successful flight that the Charlière first took to the air. The hydrogen gas was made in several barrels from which pipes ran into a large tube connected to the balloon. A venting valve was fitted in the balloon's envelope, and several bags of sand ballast were carried to control the ascent and descent of the craft.

Pilâtre de Rozier then constructed a balloon that incorporated the two tested principles. He filled the upper part of his balloon with hydrogen and the lower portion with hot air, but the open flame ignited the upper part of the sphere and de Rozier was burned to death.

The Montgolfier balloons carried an open fire in their now solidly fixed gondola, and the rise and fall of the craft was controlled by the fire, which was boosted for greater lift and damped down for reduced lift. It was a relatively safe system, and over the following years a number of improvements were made to balloons. Rubberised silk fabrics were used with nettings and bag

suspensions, a valve was mounted for the venting of gas, and oval shapes were trialled to improve directional stability and to assist in steering. Some pioneers even had recourse to oars in an effort to provide 'steerability' and with a crew of six oarsmen the Robert brothers flew, or perhaps rowed, their dirigible balloon for seven hours during 1784. Other methods of propulsion that were tried included gunpowder charges, movable wings, sails, or a rotating screw to serve as a primitive propeller.

By 1785 some 35 balloon ascents had been made, in the process taking aloft 58 passengers without mishap. However, there were tragedies in these early days, and some of the more pioneering balloonists, trying out new methods, died when their concepts failed. There was a growing business of balloon demonstrations as men toured Europe. Typical of the breed was a Frenchman, Jean-Pierre François Blanchard. He used a small balloon with a sheep tied to it, and after this had ascended he and his wife lifted off in a larger balloon and manoeuvred this to rendezvous with the smaller balloon. When the contact was made, he cut the rope holding the sheep, which floated gently to the ground under a silk parachute. The whole performance was a magnificent spectacle. Blanchard also became the first man to fly across the English Channel, from Calais to Dover.

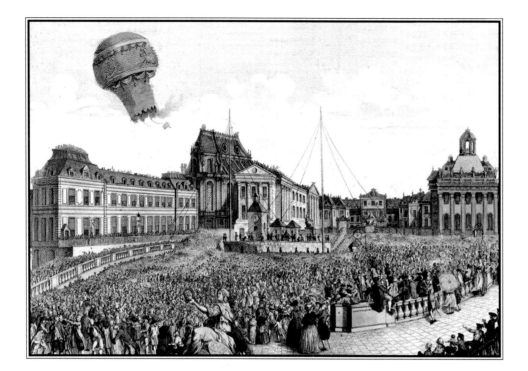

The intrepid pioneer and showman was then killed after something went wrong during his sixtieth ascent.

Oddly enough, there was a lull in balloon activities during the first part of the nineteenth century, and it was only from well into the 1800s that matters again picked up. Most important at this time was the date of 24 September 1852, when Henri Jacques Giffard successfully flew his elongated hydrogen-filled balloon in a directional flight. He used a 3-hp (2.4-kW) steam engine to drive a propeller suspended from the gondola for propulsion and steering. Giffard believed that size was important, but the engines of the period had too poor a power/weight ratio for effective airship use. In 1855 the second airship was tested, but the ship's nose rose straight into the air, the gondola became detached and remained on the ground, and the freed envelope ascended rapidly and caught fire. After laboratory experiments with hydrogen, Giffard gave up all work with this inflammable gas.

By 1868 the French government had issued no fewer than 14 patents for balloons and balloon propulsion systems. By 1874 a total of 3,700 flights had been made, including a night journey by the Frenchman Camille Flammarion, who took aloft a container filled with glow-worms for the illumination of his instruments. There had been 16 deaths among the pioneers.

In 1882, Captain Gaston Tissandier and his brother, Albert, built an airship with pointed ends, powered by an electric motor and reaching a speed of 6mph (10km/h). Two years later, the brothers were able to steer their airship to fly a figure-eight manoeuvre and land back at their starting point. In 1884, two French captains, Charles Renard and Arthur C. Krebs, constructed an airship, powered by an electric motor, and flew this at the speed of 14mph (22km/h), covering a distance of 5 miles (8km).

One of the most significant innovators was Alberto Santos-Dumont, an expatriate Brazilian living in France. He first studied and then experimented with a non-rigid spherical balloon shape in Paris. A steerable balloon in 1898, equipped with a 3.5-hp (2.6-kW) engine, ascended successfully but soon became caught in trees. Just two days later, however, there followed a successful flight. In the following year, Santos-Dumont tested balloon number 2, but the hydrogen gas contracted, the envelope shrank, and a strong gust of wind folded the envelope. Balloon number 3 worked more satisfactorily, and the inventor learned much about dirigible ballooning from it. Santos-Dumont flew number 4 at the 1900 Exposition. When Henri Deutsch offered 100,000 francs to the first person who could fly from the Aero Club around the Eiffel Tower and back within half an hour, Santos-Dumont worked diligently on steerable balloon number 5.

Having successfully rounded the Eiffel Tower, the machine flew into strong winds and was unable to land as planned. Driven back after his engine stopped, the inventor crashed the balloon into trees of the Rothschild estate. After repairs, another attempt was made, but this also ended in failure. Number 6 was built within 22 days, and with a 12-hp (8.9-kW) petrol engine the indomitable Santos-Dumont took the Deutsch prize on 19 October 1901.

### THE FIRST AIRSHIP

By this time the feasibility of heavier-than-air flight was being proved in Germany by the successful gliding experiment of Otto Lilienthal. Von Zeppelin followed Lilienthal's work with great interest and believed that in the longer term heavier-than-air craft could well become very significant. In the shorter term, however, he felt that the way forward lay with lighter-than-air craft. In 1892, von Zeppelin employed a young engineer named Theodor Kober to assist him in the planning of an airship. There was virtually no bank of data on which the two men could draw, so the whole process of designing and building an airship had to be undertaken on an empirical basis.

Kober was perhaps as technically experienced in the lighter-than-air science as anyone, for he had worked at the Riedinger balloon factory in Augsburg, where the pioneering but largely unsuccessful airship of Karl Wölfert had been built. Von Zeppelin and Kober undertook the tasks of testing the features required in a dirigible airship. Studies were made with an engine coupled to different types of propellers attached to the sides of a boat. Other tests were not as apparently strange as those made with the propellers. The correct weight distribution of the gondolas under the airship was clearly of great import, and two gondolas were considered: one for the control position and the other for the powerplant. A third gondola for the passengers was earmarked for later consideration, but obviously the most important part of the programme was to design and build an

BELOW *The development of the Zeppelin airship would have been impossible without the support of high-ranking persons in Germany. The Graf von Zeppelin is seen here (without headgear) welcoming royalty to view his endeavours.*

airship that could lift off and manoeuvre in the air before landing safely. The problems of a payload, in the form of passengers and/or freight, could be tackled later.

After almost three years of tests, the plans for an airship were complete. It was estimated that the *Luftschiff* ('airship') would cost about 300,000 marks to build on a production-line basis, but that the prototype might well exceed 1 million marks. Other problems to be faced were the lack of a hall large enough for construction, the absence of facilities for the manufacture of many of the components, and the need for a movable, floating hangar to accommodate the airship and turn into the wind for take-off. Von Zeppelin appreciated that the capital cost would be far greater than his own resources could afford, so he hoped to gain the interest of the German government. This hope proved fruitless.

In the absence of governmental support, von Zeppelin decided to appeal straight to the Emperor with the suggestion that a commission be established to test the feasibility of his concept and submit its findings to the government. On the first day of 1894, such a commission was in fact set up under the chairmanship of Professor Hermann von Helmholtz. Von Zeppelin felt sure that a scientist of the stature of von Helmholtz would soon be persuaded of the soundness of his ideas, and was therefore bitterly disappointed when the commission reported that it did not believe that the idea of a dirigible airship merited any government involvement.

*The LZ5 suffered a landing accident at Göppingen in 1909, and in the process received major damage to the nose section of the hull, which was buckled down and to starboard.*

# CHAPTER TWO

# First Commercial Flights

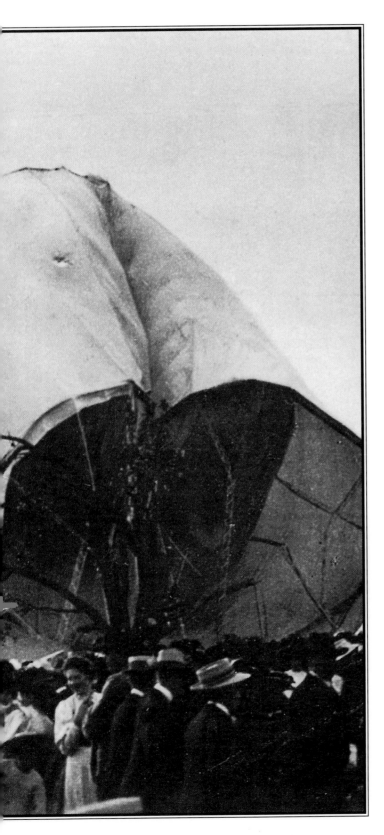

In 1896 at Stuttgart, the Graf von Zeppelin addressed an invited audience, including dignitaries and members of the government as well as technical experts, outlining his airship plans. Shortly after this, von Zeppelin wrote a long note to the Society of German Engineers: 'My observations are confined basically to the practical application of theories that are already known in the newest branch of technical science, namely aeronautics.'

Asking for consideration by the society, von Zeppelin suggested that he was right in his basic thinking, but added that he would be grateful for any correction. The society considered von Zeppelin's note, and in October issued a favourable report and suggested that the society's directorate aid in the creation of the airship. Thus, on the last day of 1896, the society issued a public statement backing von Zeppelin and encouraging the public to contribute financially toward the construction of an airship. Early in the following year, the society created a team to help the delighted von Zeppelin in the design and construction of a dirigible airship.

In August 1898 a patent, backdated to the end of August 1895, was issued to the Graf von Zeppelin for a 'steerable air vehicle with several carrying bodies arranged behind each other'. A companion illustration showed a long cylindrical airship, with eight more illustrations showing the framework and other details. The airship in question had three parts. The first, pointed at the front and flat at the rear, supported the engine in an underslung gondola. The second, which was flat at each end, carried the payload (freight or passengers). The third, flat at its front and pointed at its rear, also carried freight. All three of the sections were rigid and connected to each other by a flexible joint. Each

of the three sections had smaller inside cells (made of cloth) for the hydrogen. The framework was made up of cylindrical rings and longitudinal members, all made of aluminium alloy and skinned with cloth.

The wide publicity given to the project in newspapers all over Germany resulted in a spate of public donations sufficient for the establishment of the Aktien-Gesellschaft zur Förderung der Luftschiffahrt (Company for the Furthering of Airship Travel) in Stuttgart with a capital of about 800,000 marks. The pri-mary objective of the new company was the completion of the vital tests not yet undertaken and the establishment of a fully equipped manufacturing facility at a site yet to be chosen. The selected site was the village of Manzell near Friedrichshafen on the Bodensee (Lake Constance), a location that provided access to a large and completely flat area for flight trials, and also possessed weather (and in particular wind) that was more even than could be provided by any other region considered.

### CONSTRUCTION BEGINS

After the task of completing the drawings and preparatory plans, Theodor Kober was entrusted with the task of building the airship. The basic elements of von Zeppelin's original thinking were retained, and the resulting prototype was therefore very large with a comparatively streamlined shape, framework of aluminium alloy, separate gas cells, and external gondolas that were permanently attached and had access to the framework. Although many of these features were not new in theory, some had not been put into practice before. For instance, the separate gas cells had been postulated by August Wilhelm Zachariae in 1807, but had not previously been adopted.

The very large quantity of aluminium alloy needed for the framework could be provided by only one German company, Karl Berg of Eveking, and in overall terms the Zeppelin team needed what were for the time vast quantities of aluminium alloy for the tubular girders and other parts of the framework. The aluminium alloy parts were manufactured and initially assembled at Eveking, then disassembled and moved by rail to Friedrichshafen for reassembly and use. Problems with the delivery of other specialised materials were also encountered.

A combined workshop and hangar of considerable size was built in 1898, and on 17 June there began the construction of the airship which, it was hoped, could start on its trials in the summer of 1899 and demonstrate sufficient technical success to generate new funding, perhaps even from the government,

as much of the initial capital had already been expended. The rigid framework of the new airship was completed in November 1899, and the installation of the gas cells, which had caused some difficulty, followed a few days later. However, the fact that the turning mechanism of the movable floating launch/recovery platform had been damaged, albeit only slightly, combined with the unpredictable weather of the season to persuade Zeppelin to postpone the initial trials until the following year.

### MAIDEN FLIGHT

The prototype airship's maiden flight did not in fact take place until 2 July 1900, a day predicted as cloudless and windless. With everything checked and double-checked, and a large crowd watching from the lake's shore, the Graf von Zeppelin walked out onto the launch/recovery platform, said a prayer and boarded the control gondola with the Baron von Bassus and Eugen Wolff, together with the mechanics Eisele and Goss. Finally, the nose of the yellow-coloured airship moved slowly out of its hangar over the placid water, its body resting securely

on the long, floating launch/recovery platform, before the airship lifted almost imperceptibly from the platform at 8.03 a.m. As soon as the airship was clear of the platform, to which it was still attached by ropes, the engines were started, the propellers began to rotate, and the ropes were cast off. The airship moved away from the launch site under its own power and accelerated as it climbed to a height of 1,300ft (400m).

Some 18 minutes later, and after a flight of some 4 miles (6.5km), the airship landed at Immenstaad, where it was collected by a steam tug and towed back to its hangar at Manzell. Despite the fact that the sliding weight system, used to create and maintain longitudinal trim, had broken, the Graf von Zeppelin publicly accounted the flight a success even though he had felt it wiser to curtail this maiden flight. In private, though, von Zeppelin appreciated that his pioneer airship had several significant defects, including its very poor controllability resulting from its lack of adequate aerodynamic surfaces for longitudinal and directional control.

The limitations of the airship could not be concealed from the more percipient of the observers, however, and the com-

mentary of several newspapers was lukewarm if not actually condemnatory. But von Zeppelin was sure that poor controllability was a problem that could rapidly be overcome, and in concert with his chief engineer, Kübler, worked on the design of a more effective elevator and rudder, while Wilhelm Maybach, the chief engineer of Daimler, remained on-hand to remedy any problems with the two Daimler engines.

Von Zeppelin felt that the basic design was correct, with his concept of a rigid framework and several separate gas cells offering significant advantages over the non-rigid type of airship with its aerodynamic shape maintained by the pressurisation of a single (and therefore vulnerable) gas cell. He was sure that all would soon come to appreciate the fact that a rigid framework ensured the continuance of the airship's aerodynamic shape, that the arrangement of separate and independent gas cells ensured that any loss of gas would not cause the collapse, and that the rigid framework ensured that optimum controllability would be provided and maintained once the right control surfaces had been designed, built and incorporated. Thus the core arrangement of the Zeppelin airship, with 17 separate gas cells

ABOVE *The lattice framework of the LZ6 is seen here during erection, with the circular members connected by means of longerons in a structure braced by wires for adequate rigidity before the installation of the gas cells.*

inside a framework covered with taught fabric, was not altered. Von Zeppelin was also confident that the air between the outer cover and the gas cells minimised the temperature change inside the airship, and therefore minimised temperature-induced alteration of the volume of the lifting gas, which had to be vented if it exceeded the capacity of its cell.

Von Zeppelin was also aware that the weight of the framework meant that the size of his airship had to be sufficiently large to reduce the weight/lift ratio and thus increase its payload. The bow and stern were both tapered for reduced drag and thus improved speed, and the length/beam ratio of 11.64/1 (420 x 36ft [128 x 11m]) produced a long cigar-like hull that also helped to minimise drag and the effects of crosswinds. The two engines and their propellers were located close to the hull so that the propellers' thrust would be generated as near as possible to the whole assembly's centre of gravity. In overall terms, therefore, the Graf von Zeppelin believed that there was nothing fundamentally wrong with his LZ1 (Luftschiff Zeppelin 1), though clearly a more effective method of longitudinal control was required.

## A DIFFICULT START

Two more test flights were undertaken. On 17 October the LZ1 lifted off on its second flight, and the improved steering mechanism was soon seen to provide much better response to control demands, allowing a higher level of agility in the air. The flight lasted about 80 minutes, in the course of which a maximum speed of 18mph (29km/h) was recorded by comparison with the first flight's maximum speed of 8mph (13km/h). On 24 October the LZ1 departed on its third test flight, but this effort was largely stymied by the strength of the wind, which was too high for the underpowered LZ1 to make effective headway. The flight lasted just 23 minutes.

It was a moment of crisis for von Zeppelin, for virtually all of the available funds had been spent, and were insufficient to buy more hydrogen. In the absence of further donated funds, the Graf von Zeppelin therefore had to agree to the liquidation of the undertaking. The airship and its hangar were dismantled, and the sum of 120,000 marks realised from the liquidation was used to pay off at least some of the creditors.

Von Zeppelin was heartbroken, but in January of the following year delivered a lecture to the German Colonial Association, which elicited a warm response as well as further recognition in the form of a decoration and an appreciative letter from Kaiser Wilhelm II. Von Zeppelin then wrote to the Kaiser, but received no further communication. He decided to appeal once more to the Society of German Engineers, which agreed to establish another committee to look at all aspects of airship construction. The committee pointed out that the semi-rigid type of airship offered considerable military advantages, inasmuch as it could more easily be dismantled for rail movement and was also, it was claimed, less sensitive to crosswinds. Although there were dissenting points of view, the committee generally came down against the rigid airship, and the Graf von Zeppelin therefore had recourse to a final appeal in a mass-circulation newspaper, in which the most telling point for the design and manufacture of a new rigid airship was the need to bolster Germany's technological display at the world fair due to be held at St Louis in the USA. The newspaper's readers contributed 55,000 marks, and another 124,500 marks came from a lottery. A final 12,500 marks arrived in the form of a discretionary donation by the chancellor, Bernhard von Bülow.

### STARTING AGAIN

A new manufacturing and operations shed was built on land near the Bodensee donated by the city of Friedrichshafen, and it was here that the LZ2 began to take shape. The new airship was generally similar to the LZ1 but incorporated several major improvements, including the powerplant of two 85- rather than 32-hp (63- rather than 24-kW) Daimler engines, and the use in the framework of triangular rather than tubular girders for a greater strength/weight ratio.

The LZ2 was completed in October 1905, and despite the fears of the Graf von Zeppelin about the weather, which can be very unpredictable at this time of the year, was readied for its first flight on 30 November. The lake's water level was too low for the floating platform to be used in launching the airship, so the two engine gondolas were located on pontoons and a launch towed the airship out of the hangar. The gusting wind then resulted in an accident in which the airship's covering was torn in several places, and all thoughts of starting the flight test programme during this period of adverse weather were then cancelled, work being concentrated on repairs.

The advent of better weather led to the rescheduling of the maiden flight for 17 January 1906. At first all went well, but then both of the airship's engines stopped and the now-drifting LZ2 was driven downwind to the northeast before achieving a moderately successful landing. However, during the night a storm resulted in the LZ2 being damaged beyond economic repair. This could again have led to the end of the Graf von Zeppelin's career as the pioneer of rigid airships, but the German government allowed a national lottery to raise further funds, and further contributions came from a national subsidy, a state lottery in Württemberg, and a loan from the Committee for the Study of Motorised Airship Navigation.

BELOW *The LZ6, notable like other early Zeppelin airships for the complexity of its tail surfaces with their multitude of control elements, is carefully manoeuvred into the floating hangar.*

ABOVE *The Deutschland II civil airship in flight during 1911.*

RIGHT *The Deutschland II was destroyed in an accident at Düsseldorf in 1911.*

The German government also provided the funding for the construction of a new airship manufacturing and operations facility of its own design.

## A NATIONAL HERO

The result of this effort was the LZ3, which was again a development of the basic Zeppelin concept. This improved airship made its maiden flight in September 1907 in front of many senior government officials, who were generally very impressed by the performance and handling of the airship, which returned to its lift-off point after its flight. There were many other flights in the weeks that followed, and the LZ3 proved itself a capable airship that could stay aloft for periods of up to 8 hours at a time. The success of the airship inaugurated a period of great esteem for the Graf von Zeppelin, whose opponents were generally army officers of low rank and with interests in non-rigid airships. The period also saw the arrival of one of the great figures in Zeppelin airship history, Hugo Eckener. This young man was an economist working as a journalist for the *Frankfurter Zeitung* newspaper, which was somewhat critical of the Graf von Zeppelin and his undertakings. Von Zeppelin invited Eckener to talk with him and look over the Friedrichshafen facility, and as a result Eckener became a convert to the concept of the rigid airship.

Von Zeppelin was now the object of what was almost national hysteria, even receiving a congratulatory letter from the Kaiser on the occasion of his 69th birthday. He capitalised on this to request funds for the construction of other airships. The German government responded with an initial subsidy of 400,000 marks. At von Zeppelin's further request, a reimbursement of 500,000 marks was given to replenish his own fortune after his earlier personal funding of the airship development.

By the end of 1907 von Zeppelin was famous throughout Germany and in an excellent position to capitalise on the technical success of the LZ3 with the design and construction of a new and still more capable airship, the LZ4. The design for the airship included a length of 446ft (136m) and a diameter of 42ft (13m) for a gas capacity of 519,000ft³ (14,500m³). Power was to be provided yet again by two engines, although in this instance each generating 104hp (78kW). Other changes were the increased length/beam ratio of 10.63/1, which was intended to reduce drag and thus boost speed, but also resulted in too whippy a hull structure, and an observation position (connected to the forward gondola by an external walkway) in the extreme bow.

The LZ4's first flight was scheduled for 20 June 1908, and was completed with total success under the personal supervision of von Zeppelin. A second flight followed on 23 June, the airship remaining airborne for more than two hours on this occasion, and a third flight was made on 29 June, when the airship returned to base after a flight of more than six hours.

### SAFETY REFINEMENTS

Von Zeppelin was now in considerable demand as a lecturer, and on 25 January 1908 had told his Berlin audience about his overall concept of the rigid airship. There were three things required, von Zeppelin averred, for safe flight in an airship: first, there had to be at least two independent engines so that in the event that one engine failed, the second would still be available to provide sufficient manoeuvrability; second, a completely rigid hull was needed to ensure effective controllability; and third, the size of the airship had to be sufficiently large to permit the carriage of a sizeable fuel load as a means of ensuring sustained power if and when a flight had to be extended because of unforeseen circumstances, such as weather conditions.

Von Zeppelin also suggested that speed was a secondary consideration in relation to safety, and that safety should be increased by the adoption of improved navigational aids to provide for continued safe flight in adverse weather conditions (especially clouds and fog) and at night. He also pointed out that the availability of the small bow platform made it possible to improve navigational accuracy by celestial navigation, and that while sufficient space was available in current airships for the carriage of passengers, greater space and comfort would be provided in later designs, which would be capable of 37mph (60km/h) and have sufficient fuel for a range of 1,900 miles (3,060km) covered in two days at a high cruising speed, or 3,700 miles (6,000km) covered in four-and-a-half days at a lower cruising speed.

Von Zeppelin further suggested that hangars would no longer have to be built so that they could be rotated to face into the wind, and suggested that a regular airship service linking Berlin with Copenhagen could be established for as little as 1 million marks and generate a 10 per cent return on the investment. Perhaps more practically, in the longer term, von Zeppelin told his audience that the airship had great potential in military and naval affairs. This military and naval utility was initially seen in terms of reconnaissance, allowing commanders to gain useful tactical data about an enemy from an airship operating at an altitude above the effective ceiling of the light weapons that might currently be brought to bear on it. The German pioneer of rigid airship operations also claimed that his type of airship would also be useful for exploration.

### THE SCHWEIZERFAHRT

More than happy with LZ4's initial series of successful flights, von Zeppelin now started to lay the first part of a plan for a 24-hour flight, which he felt would wholly vindicate the notion of an airship as a fully practical means of transport. Given the importance of such a flight as an undertaking that might break as well as make the concept of the rigid airship, von Zeppelin decided that the first step should be a 12-hour flight. This became the so-called *Schweizerfahrt* ('journey over Switzerland'). In excellent weather conditions for the undertaking, the official party was carried to the waiting airship in a launch and boarded the forward gondola, where members of the ground crew had been waiting until they embarked, in order that the airship would maintain the proper balance. In the forward gondola were von Zeppelin, Professor Hugo Hergesell of the German Ministry of the Interior, Ludwig Dürr (chief engineer), two steering engineers, and six other engineers. The so-called salon, actually a small cabin located between the two gondolas in the centreline keel under the hull, accommodated the writer Emil Sandt. A few minutes after the passengers had taken their places, the LZ4 lifted off and headed toward Konstanz.

Specially selected for promotional purposes, the route took the airship over many towns and villages so that as many people as possible could see the LZ4. However, when the weather started to worsen over the Wallensee, the course was altered to take the airship to Winterthur and over Thurgau. The LZ4 flew at a speed of almost 40mph (65km/h) and reached an altitude of about 2,400ft (730m) over the mountainous terrain, demonstrating first-class performance over the difficult areas with tricky air currents. In overall terms, the LZ4 flew over Konstanz, Schaffhausen, then along the Rhine and Aar rivers to Lucerne, Zug, Zürich and Winterthur, before returning to Friedrichshafen via Frauenfeld, Romanshorn, Rorschach, Bregenz and Lindau, the overall flight time being slightly more than 12 hours.

The *Schweizerfahrt* generated enormous interest in and enthusiasm for the Zeppelin airship, and von Zeppelin received a congratulatory telegram from the German crown prince. The sales of Zeppelin memorabilia rose to unprecedented levels, the administration of Berlin renamed a square Zeppelin Platz, Frankfurt am Main renamed a long park area between two wide avenues as the Zeppelin Anlagen, and Donaueschingen became the first of many German towns to rename a street as the Zeppelinstrasse. The success of the *Schweizerfahrt* was also responsible for a rapid growth in the general belief in the safety of airship travel, a fact reflected in the growing numbers of prominent persons arriving at Friedrichshafen for a flight: notable among them were the King and Queen of Württemberg, who took a flight over the Schwabian lakes on 3 July 1907.

### THE FIRST 24-HOUR ENDURANCE FLIGHT

At this time the Gross and Basenach aircraft was totally destroyed near Berlin, but this did not seem to affect adversely the generally high estimation of the Zeppelin airship. Even though there were a number of opponents, both private and official, to the concept of the rigid airship, the general belief was that the Zeppelin airship was totally safe.

Given the high esteem in which he was currently held, von Zeppelin decided that the time was right for the 24-hour endurance flight. This was scheduled for the beginning of July 1908, and von Zeppelin himself would be in command. However, his plans were disrupted by the advent of his 70th birthday on 8 July, which resulted in a spate of honours, eulogies and official as well as private celebrations culminating in a major firework display. This delay meant that the 24-hour flight had to be rescheduled first for 14 July 1908 and then, after two separate accidents in which the airship was damaged as it was being towed out of its hangar, for 4 August 1908.

On the morning of this day the LZ4 lifted off in good order and set off along the flight route fixed by von Zeppelin to offer a sight of the airship to as many Germans as possible as it passed over the Schaffhausen falls and then proceeded down the Rhine. The airship passed Basle at 9.30 a.m. and Strasbourg at 12.30 p.m., and approached Darmstadt at 4.30 p.m. Soon after it had

ABOVE *The civil airship Schwaben, here shortly after lifting off*
*on a commercial passenger-carrying flight during 1911.*
*The airship was beginning to reach an early level of maturity.*

passed Darmstadt, however, matters started to take a turn for the worse as the oil pressure of the forward engine started to drop and the engine's temperature climbed. Conscious of safety rather than promotional success, von Zeppelin decided that the LZ4 should land so that repairs could be effected. The LZ4 touched down at Nierstein near Oppenheim on the Rhine, and a large crowd soon gathered as the repairs were completed and the airship lifted off once more.

This unplanned landing delayed the progress of the flight, and as a result it was midnight when the airship finally approached the city of Mainz, where the LZ4's course was redirected south with more than half of the planned course completed. Over Mannheim, however, there was another problem with the same engine, where a connecting rod bearing had burnt out. Von Zeppelin decided this time that the airship should not land as such an operation at night and in an unknown place with untrained ground support would be dangerous in the extreme. The other engine was throttled back to run more comfortably, and the LZ4 got as far as Stuttgart, some 75 miles (120km) away, where a perfect landing was effected at sunrise at nearby Echterdingen. At this time von Zeppelin's main worry was that the day would probably be hot, and that the loss of gas during the previous day, which had also been hot, could cause problems with inadequate lift when they set off again.

Police and troops had to be used to keep an eager crowd well back from the airship so that the crew could undertake

the necessary repairs without hindrance, and von Zeppelin went to a nearby inn for breakfast and then, pending word that the repairs had been completed, lunch. During this time the wind began to rise, although all concerned with the running of the airship felt that there was no cause for concern as the LZ4 was well moored, and as the troops were helping to hold the airship down. Von Zeppelin was looking forward to lifting off early in the afternoon, and though disappointed that the 24-hour flight had not been possible, was content that the airship had in general behaved well. Then there was a huge blast, followed by screams from the crowd: the LZ4 was nothing but a mass of flame.

It was later established that at 2.50 p.m. a gust of wind had hit the airship broadside on, the process lifting the stern and sending the airship about 500ft (150m) up into the air, when it was carried south as it descended and hit a stand of trees, catching fire and exploding. It is likely that the fire and explosion were caused by a loss of gas as the airship was lifted off the ground, followed by its ignition by a discharge of static electricity in the miniature but potent storm that caused the accident. Many men lost their lives in the accident, and von Zeppelin was rendered totally distraught. Returning to Friedrichshafen, he was minded to order an immediate cessation of all Zeppelin work to remove the need for an official decree. The whole of the German-speaking world seemed to come to the support of the Graf von Zeppelin, whose home and office were inundated with letters and telegrams of support, money, and visitors from right across the social spectrum. So great was the tidal wave of support that a *Reichskomitee zur Aufbringung des nationalen Luftschiffsbau-Fonds für Graf von Zeppelin* (State Committee to Raise the National Airship Building Fund for the Graf von Zeppelin) was created.

As his grief about the catastrophe began to abate, von Zeppelin was both touched and encouraged by the response of Germany, in the form of both its institutions and its people. Despite the financial and human cost of the tragedy, he soon learned, there were still only a few voices raised against the idea of the rigid airship, and the money eventually received totalled somewhat more than six-and-a-quarter million marks. This allowed both the resumption and expansion of airship-building operations by an organisation that was revised into two halves with the Zeppelin-Stiftung as the financial element under Ernst

Uhland and the Luftschiffsbau-Zeppelin as the airship-building element under Alfred Colsman, with von Zeppelin as chairman of the whole undertaking.

## PICKING UP THE PIECES

Given the enlarged size of the Zeppelin organisation in its new form, a larger site was required and Friedrichshafen soon made it possible for the organisation to purchase the required land. The Graf von Zeppelin then organised a national contest for the design of the new hangar. Of the 68 design submissions, the best was judged to be that of the Brückenbau Flender company of Benrath, a specialist in the design and construction of bridges, to whom the contract was awarded for a huge hangar able to accommodate two airships in a volume 603ft (184m) long, 151ft (46m) wide and 75ft (23m) high.

BELOW *Refinements in airship operation were no guarantee against accident, as the loss of the Schwaben testified in 1912. The large window-opening in the wrecked gondola gives an idea of the superb view passengers would have enjoyed.*

At this stage of the effort, the Graf von Zeppelin envisaged the side-by-side but separate operation of three units devoted to passenger, military and naval airships, even though the German navy had as yet to express any interest in the airship. As the building of the new hangar proceeded, the LZ3 was renovated so that von Zeppelin could undertake demonstration flights and thereby keep the rigid airship in the minds of the public and, just as importantly, of high-ranking persons. As a result the count gave flights to several members of the various German royal families. Other highlights of this period included the carriage, on 29 March 1909, of 25 persons on a single flight and, on 6 April of the same year, a non-stop flight of 12 hours 27 minutes.

Many of the LZ3's subsequent flights were made from February 1909 under the command of Major Sperling, an army officer based at Friedrichshafen with his aeronautical detachment (four officers and 120 other ranks). Intensive training was undertaken before making flights in the airship. During March and April, the military detachment undertook 17 training flights, all of them completed without incident of any kind. By this time the LZ3 had flown 45 times, in the process covering a distance of 2,733 miles (4,398km).

Sperling took over the LZ3 officially for the military on 29 June 1909 and the airship, now renamed as the Z I, was ordered to Germany's western frontier to watch over the fortress area of Metz. On the way to its new base the Z I encountered heavy rain, and Sperling ordered an overnight halt at Mittelbiberach, where in fact the Z I remained for another three days after another day of rain and two days of drying out, before setting off for the new base. The German army bought no other airship until 1911.

## DELAG

The next major date in the development of the Zeppelin airship as a means of transport came on 19 November 1909, when the Deutsche Luftschiffahrts-Aktiengesellschaft (German Airship Travel Corporation), or 'Delag' for short, was created, with Eckener as its managing director, to plan and operate regular airship transport routes across key parts of Germany. Delag, a Luftschiffsbau-Zeppelin subsidiary, was a limited stock company with a capital of 3 million marks, 500,000 marks of which were invested by the Zeppelin-Stiftung.

The new company's aim was not merely to promote airship travel but also to order airships from the Zeppelin construction company. Delag soon ordered two Zeppelin airships with which it would begin passenger services between selected cities, and work soon started on the construction of suitable airship- and passenger-handling facilities outside the cities that would be served by the new routes.

With the prospect of larger orders in the offing, the Luftschiffsbau-Zeppelin was concerned to ensure that there would be no bottlenecks in its production programme as a result of problems in the manufacture of essential components by subcontractors, and therefore established a number of its own subsidiaries. The task of designing and building engines optimised for airship use was allocated to Karl Maybach, son of Daimler's chief engineer Wilhelm Maybach, who had supplied the earliest engines. The new Maybach engine, which had a specially developed lightweight cooling system and a safer carburettor, was a six-cylinder inline unit developing 150hp (112kW). The Luftfahrzeug-Motorenbau GmbH, later renamed as the Maybach Motorenbau, was created on 23 March 1909 with a production facility planned at Bissingen an der Enz.

Other companies were subsequently founded to supply the special needs of the Zeppelin manufacturing effort. For instance, the discovery that the friction of the type of rubberised cotton fabric used for the skin of gas cells could lead to the sparking that might ignite the entire cover when the airship came to rest on the ground and the cell collapsed, led to the search for an alternative and safer material. The selected material was *Goldschlägerhaut* ('goldbeater's skin') derived from cattle intestines, so in 1912 Zeppelin bought the company that produced this material, the B.G. Textile Werke GmbH of Berlin-Tempelhof, and renamed it as the Ballonhüllen-Gesellschaft. Then in the following year the parent company established the Zeppelin-Hallenbau GmbH of Berlin to construct Zeppelin hangars, and in the same year the Zeppelin-Wasserstoff und Sauerstoffwerke AG of Staaken assumed the responsibility of manufacturing the hydrogen required as the airships' lifting gas.

After a Swiss engineer, Max Naag, had developed a system of machining gears with considerable precision, Zeppelin founded the Zahnradfabrik AG during 1915 in Friedrichshafen to produce these important items, which were essential for the transfer of power from the engines to the propellers and other auxiliary machinery but up to this time had been prone to considerable unreliability.

### FLYING FURTHER AFIELD

One of von Zeppelin's longer-term plans for the exploitation of airship transport had been in the exploration role, and in June 1910 the Deutsche Arktische Zeppelin Expedition sailed from Kiel to investigate the feasibility of using an airship for arctic exploration. At Tromsö, the party trans-shipped to the small arctic steamer *Fönix* to sail for Spitsbergen, the island from which three balloonists led by Salomon André had made their ascent in 1897 in an unsuccessful and fatal effort to drift over the North Pole to America.

The party made several ascents in a balloon that had been bought for that purpose, and von Zeppelin was as active as the others in undertaking the balloon ascents and travelled by dog sled in an effort to find a site suitable for a Zeppelin hangar. No arctic expedition by airship was attempted at the time, but the expedition had led von Zeppelin to decide that the rigid airship was generally suitable for the task, and also for long trans-oceanic crossings. This fact finally caught the attention of the German navy, which ordered its first airship in 1912.

However, when there was no flood of orders for military and/or naval airships, the Zeppelin organisation decided to concentrate its efforts on passenger-carrying airships. The company approached numerous cities with the suggestion that the creation of a landing field and hangar would make them regular stops on the transport network that Zeppelin was planning as a means of linking Germany's most important industrial and financial centres. As a result, landing fields were developed in Baden-Baden (Oos), Berlin (Johannisthal), Dresden, Düsseldorf, Frankfurt am Main, Gotha, Hamburg, Leipzig and Potsdam, and the Hamburg-Amerika Linie was appointed as the company's ticket agent.

During its first year of operations, Delag made 41 passenger flights, lasting a total of 86 hours. In 1912 almost 500 flights were completed, rising in 1913 to 773 flights totalling 1,100 or more hours. The routes were between cities, initially from Hamburg to Schleswig-Holstein, and from Düsseldorf to Baden-Baden by way of Frankfurt. Others city pairings followed in short order as landing facilities were completed. The airships were naturally no match to the speedier railway trains, but for leisurely trips across the country they proved very popular despite the fact that their fares were considerably higher than those of even first-class services on trains: the round-trip fare between Hamburg and Schleswig-Holstein was 200 marks. Even so, large numbers of Germans undertook Zeppelin trips for the excitement of floating, apparently without support, high in the air with a superb view below.

For obvious reasons, safety was the primary consideration in the Delag managers' minds, and in the event of a conflict between passengers' safety and the possibility of weather-induced danger, the final decision was always in favour of safety. As a general rule, moreover, each new Zeppelin airship had a feature or features intended to improve safety by comparison with its predecessor.

It was at this time that names replaced the earlier alphanumeric system as the means of designating Zeppelin airships. For instance, the LZ7 became the Deutschland, and other Zeppelin airships were the Hansa, Sachsen, Schwaben and Viktoria Luise, the last named in honour of the Kaiserin.

### EARLY TRAGEDIES

Despite a programme of steady improvement, the safety record of the Zeppelin airships was by no means perfect. In 1910 the Deutschland had to undertake an emergency landing during a severe storm in the Teutoburger Wald region, and was destroyed on the ground after the passengers had disembarked. On 31 May 1909, while it was travelling toward Berlin, the LZ5 flew into a tree near Göppingen after having been in the air for 38 hours. Exhausted, Captain Dürr and his crew slept on the ground below the Zeppelin and then reboarded the airship to return to the hangar. The damage to the stern of the LZ5, suffered in the landing accident, apparently had no effect on its airworthiness: the captain had ordered the damaged portion of the framework to be cut off and the hole thus exposed to be covered with the now superfluous tail covering, the ends of which were tied over the opening. The front gas cell had also been punctured, but this did not harm the airship's overall buoyancy. The incident was further proof, had it been needed, of the superior survivability of the rigid airship, for a semi-rigid airship would have lost all its lifting gas.

The tenth Zeppelin airship was the Schwaben, and after carrying 1,553 passengers in the course of 218 incident-free flights, this airship was lost on 28 June 1912 after an explosion and subsequent fire that cost the lives of 39 passengers and members of the crew.

Von Zeppelin was generally unhappy at the disinterest of the military and naval authorities to his airships, but in addition felt slighted when all of the different systems of airship construction were lumped together by the military and naval authorities, especially as it had repeatedly been shown that each of the types (rigid, semi-rigid and non-rigid) had wholly different properties. It should be noted in this context that there was a rival company in the design and construction of rigid airships in the form of the Luftfahrzeugbau Schütte-Lanz of Mannheim-Rheinau. The designer was Dr Franz Schütte of Danzig and the first airship was built in 1911.

The Schütte-Lanz airships had a greater length/beam ratio than the Zeppelin airships, and were more streamlined, had a gas capacity of some 699,225ft³ (19,800m³), and had their control surfaces hinged to the trailing edges of their tail-mounted fixed surfaces in an arrangement radically cleaner and more successful than the boxlike features typical of the Zeppelin airships' controls. The earlier Schütte-Lanz airships had a framework based on a geodetic arrangement of triangular wooden girders, but later airships from this stable had a more conventional framework, still of wood, with transverse frames and longerons. The engines also drove their propellers directly, thus eliminating the elaborately conceived and often troublesome system of gears and shafts typical of Zeppelin practice. Another distinctive feature was the placement of the keel inside instead of outside the hull, as was the case with Zeppelin airships. During the nine years of its existence, however, Schütte-Lanz completed only 22 airships.

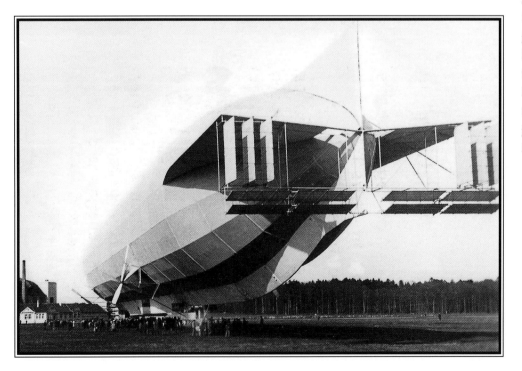

LEFT *As revealed by this photograph of the Sachsen in 1913, it was essential that the inflammable hydrogen gas be located in gondolas outside the hull, from which the propellers were driven via long shafts.*

*The conning positions in the control gondola below the forward part of the airship*
*(in this instance the LZ127) provided the crew with superb fields of vision.*

# CHAPTER THREE

# Travelling in Style

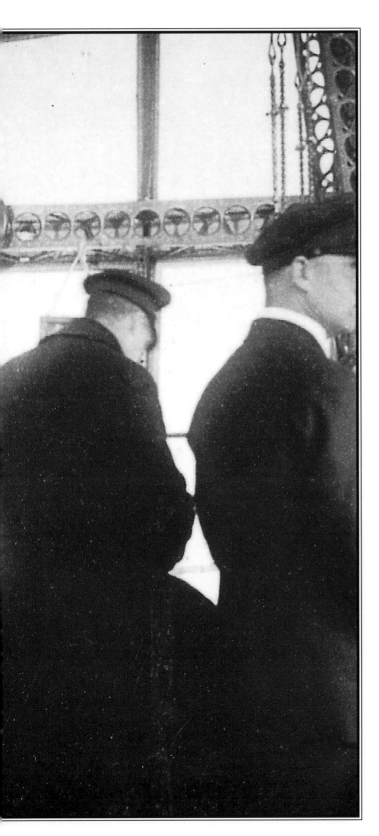

In the 35 years during which Zeppelin airships were designed, beginning with the LZ1 of 1899 and ending with the LZ129 of 1934, the engineers at the Zeppelin company faced and overcame a host of problems both large and small.

In the report that the Graf von Zeppelin had sent to the King of Württemberg in 1887 about the desirability and feasibility of the lighter-than-air craft, this great pioneer stated that the evolution of the airship into a vehicle offering practical capabilities in the military arena demanded that it had to be capable of navigation in the face of strong air currents so that it could be directed at the intent of its commander rather than the whim of the wind. The airship had to be able to remain in the air for a period of at least 24 hours so that it could fly from its base to the region it was to reconnoitre or bomb and then return to its base. Moreover it needed to possess the structural strength not only to survive adverse weather but also to lift a heavy 'usable' load of items, such as the crew, supplies of water and fuel for the operation of the airship, as well as consumables for the crew and military equipment, such as weapons, ammunition, cameras etc. In overall terms, therefore, von Zeppelin had concluded that the practical airship would have to be large.

Drawing on the most advanced technical thinking of the period, the design of the LZ1 was therefore created to provide the greatest possible load-carrying ability, the highest possible reliability and the fastest possible speed. The airship's gas capacity of 399,000ft³ (11,300m³) was enormous by the standards of the day, and so too were its primary external dimensions, which included a length of 420ft (128m) and a diameter of 38ft (12m). The shaping of the hull was based more on practical aspects of the manufacturing capabilities available than on purely aerodynamic considerations, which were in any event comparatively little understood at the time, and the hull was therefore essentially cylindrical in shape with tapered bow and stern sections.

The constant section of the hull's main section allowed the use of identical frames, which eased the design and production process, and also facilitated the replacement of any frame should it be damaged. In structural terms, therefore, the hull was based on an assembly of 16 identical 24-facet ring frames spaced at 26-ft (8-m) intervals, and connected by longerons to create a core structure that was covered with fabric. The lifting gas which, in the absence of anything else, was hydrogen, was carried inside 17 separate cloth cells installed between the ring frames, and special care was taken to ensure that there was some air between the surface of the gas cells and the airship's outer skin. The object of this feature was to provide an insulation layer that would mitigate the effect of the sun's heating of the outer skin on the gas cells in an effort to avoid the hydrogen becoming heated, which would then expand and have to be vented, thereby reducing the lift available when the temperature dropped and also entailing additional cost as the cells would have to be replenished before any subsequent flight.

Propulsion of the airship was entrusted to a pair of Daimler N1899 petrol engines each delivering 14hp (10kW) and powering an arrangement of four propellers. In performance terms this translated as a maximum speed of 17.5mph (28km/h), although it was only very seldom that a speed of 7.5mph (12km/h) was exceeded in practice. The engines were located in separate gondolas connected by a long 'keel', itself attached to the underside of the airship proper by means of trusses and wires. Control of the airship in the horizontal and vertical planes was achieved by deflection of control surfaces at the front and the rear of the airship's hull, and fore-and-aft movement of a weight attached by wires to the front and rear of the 'keel' unit was employed to alter the longitudinal attitude of the airship in the air. The gondolas were themselves open and provided accommodation for a maximum of five persons. They were of watertight construction so that the airship could rise or land on the water and, to provide for any landing on solid ground, had a spring-mounted rubber bumper under each of the gondolas to cushion the vertical impact of the landing.

## NEW FEATURES

The pioneering LZ1 introduced six features that were not altered in later Zeppelin airships although they were, of course, subjected to constant improvement and refinement as dictated by experience as well as theoretical considerations. These elementary features were: the rigid structural framework of aluminium alloy under a covering of fabric; the use of a large number of completely separate cells for the accommodation of the lifting gas; the installation of the engines as separate and indeed independent units each with its own fuel supply; the division of the payload and other masses for car-

ABOVE *The tail cone of the LZ126, a late Zeppelin with the cruciform of tail-mounted surfaces that was by now standard in Zeppelin airships.*

RIGHT *Constructional details of the LZ1 (built in 1899) reveal how little change there was in the fundamental features of the design of the Zeppelin airship.*

riage by different parts of the airship's primary structure; the use of separate horizontal and vertical surfaces to stabilise the airship in the longitudinal and directional planes; the location of the control centre on the centreline under the airship's hull for the best possible forward and downward fields of vision.

The philosophy that remained a central plank of the Zeppelin airship concept throughout its existence was perhaps most neatly encapsulated by Ludwig Dürr, one of von Zeppelin's closest professional colleagues and the Zeppelin company's chief designer and engineer: 'We cannot change the idea or add anything to it. We can only provide some refinements.'

## MATERIALS

The material selected for use in all of the Zeppelin airships was aluminium alloy, which was selected and then retained for its high strength/weight ratio to ensure the structural integrity of a massive framework. Moreover, the framework had also, of very real necessity, to be as light as possible so that lift of the gas it contained was considerably greater that the structural weight and thereby allowed the airship to carry as much payload as possible. The material used in the airships from the Zeppelin stable in its early days, when the manufacture and use of aluminium alloys was still very much in its infancy, was a zinc/aluminium alloy modified from the time of the LZ2 by the addition of a small proportion of copper. The zinc/copper/aluminium alloy was still far from perfect in this task, however, and in its search for an improved material, the Zeppelin company first used Dural, created in 1909 by the German Alfred Wim, for parts of the LZ7

LEFT  An essential feature of the Zeppelin airship structure was the use of built-up lattice-work girders of light alloy. These could be bolted together to create all the various members required by the airship's structure.

BELOW  The interior of the Zeppelin airship may have looked like an impenetrable mess of latticework girders and wires, but the volume between the circular cross-frames was left open for the accommodation of gas cells, walkways and ladders.

during 1910. It switched to the exclusive use of Dural in the LZ26 of 1914. The Zeppelin company initially used T-section girders and L-shaped stiffeners, but in 1919 switched to pressed-section material that offered greater strength and reduced weight.

It is impossible to overestimate the importance of Dural in the development of the Zeppelin airship, and indeed in the progress of aeronautical art as represented by heavier-than-air as well as lighter-than-air craft. Dural was known to the employees of the Zeppelin company just as *Werkstoff* ('work material'), and its properties were responsible for a major improvement in the performance and the lift of the airships. In this latter capacity, the structural weight of the airship expressed as a percentage of the total lift, had improved from 78.6 per cent in the LZ1 to 65–70 per cent in the period leading up to the outbreak of World War I. It then improved fairly dramatically to 61.6 per cent in the LZ26 and then continued to drop to a figure between 20 and 30 per cent by the end of the war. In the last Zeppelin airships it remained at between 35 and 40 per cent. Dural was produced in a number of forms, and its primary constituents were copper (3.5–4.5 per cent), magnesium (0.2–0.75 per cent), manganese (0.4–1 per cent) and aluminium (at least 92 per cent).

### DESIGN REFINEMENTS

The design of the Zeppelin airship's structure was steadily refined. The spacing of the primary ring frames was increased by 6.6ft (2m) to 33ft (10m) in the LZ26 as the use of Dural allowed the use of fewer frames, and a spacing of 49ft (15m) became increasingly standard from the LZ100 of 1917. The ring frames of the LZ1 had 24 flat sides, but this figure was reduced to 16 in the LZ2, and later a type of slightly convex facets was used, which gave the outer skin the appearance of being based on smaller side panels and at the same time gave the airship a more rounded shape that was in fact considerably smoother in overall terms and thereby reduced drag.

The walkway along the underside of the airship was originally just a plank with a hand rope attached to the frame, and was used as a companion way to allow members of the crew to move up and down the length of the airship between the two gondolas. In the LZ2 this arrangement was improved into a solidly attached walkway, and in the LZ7 in 1910 the walkway was fully enclosed in the hull of the airship but still attached. Finally, from the LZ8 of 1911 the walkway became part of the structural keel and as such was an integral part of the airship's frame inside the outer covering. This concept was retained for the rest of the time the Zeppelin airships were built.

Over the primary structure of the airship's hull was the tight fabric covering that provided the surface that penetrated the air as the airship travelled. On the LZ1 this covering was of an expensive cotton fabric impregnated to make it waterproof. As lighter, stronger and cheaper fabrics became available, these were adopted for the outer skin, and the fabric was protected by a cellulose preparation, or 'dope', that both waterproofed and shrank the fabric. The 'dope' was painted directly onto the fabric and, after it had dried, was rubbed down to a smooth finish, after which another coat was applied to make the hull as slippery as possible. A feature of the process during World War I was the addition of a black aniline dye to give the Zeppelin airships what was then thought to be an effective camouflage finish for nocturnal operations. With the resumption of airship construction and operation after the war, the 'dope' included aluminium powder to create a silvery reflective finish designed to improve the insulation of the gas cells from the sun's heat and also to reflect the ultra-violet element of the sun's light that otherwise damaged the fabric.

The fabric covering was attached to the airship's structure in strips by means of hooks and eyes, and the strips were then laced together before the seams were covered with pasted-on strips of similar material. To correct the unevenness of the hull covering, wider strips were attached horizontally from the LZ92 onwards.

### POWER SOURCE

In the early days of the Zeppelin airship, the power available from the primitive petrol engines of the period was so low that the aerodynamically inefficient but constructionally simple cigar-like shape of the period's airships was of little consequence, especially as there was little operational merit perceived at the time for a high speed through the air. So it was only with the advent of more powerful engines, opening the possibility of higher speeds at a time when the commercial viability of the Zeppelin airship was beginning to become apparent, that a more fully optimised aerodynamic shaping assumed greater importance. The answer here was the streamlined shape like that of a fish, and to provide the optimum profiles along the hull of its airships the Zeppelin company turned to the Aerodynamische Versuchsanstalt (Aerodynamic Experimental Organisation) at Göttingen. The organisation provided much valuable information, and was later in the position to perform wind-tunnel tests on airship models for the provision of practical validation of different profiles. The Zeppelin company also built its own wind tunnel, at the time the largest in Germany, at Friedrichshafen for its own examination of air pressure gradients along the hull, streamlining factors, and the stresses on various parts of the airship. The effect of this aerodynamic refinement was an evolution from the basically cylindrical hull of the LZ1 to a streamlined hull of pronounced taper forward and aft of the point of maximum diameter. The stages in this process are best epitomised by the LZ40 of 1915 with an increase in diameter near the bow, the LZ62 of 1916 with a greater beam/length ratio, the LZ104 of

ABOVE *The two- and four-blade propeller units were identical in concept, although not in size, to those employed in heavier-than-air craft.*

RIGHT *Landing was controlled by means of ropes pulled by the ground crew, and a large 'bumper' under the control gondola cushioned the impact with the ground.*

1917 with a greater length/beam ratio, the LZ120 of 1919 with a shorter hull and greater beam/length ratio, and from the LZ126 of 1924 a longer hull of greater length/beam ratio.

### STRUCTURAL CONSIDERATIONS

Throughout this period the size of the Zeppelin airships, with the exception of the LZ120, increased steadily, for the greater the internal volume of the hull, the greater the volume of the gas cells that could be incorporated and thus the greater the lift that could be provided. Size, and the structural considerations that went along with it, was arguably the single most important consideration in the development of the Zeppelin airship for both civil and military applications, even though these demanded a number of different features: in civil airships, for example, maximisation of the payload/range parameter was all important whereas a very high speed and good altitude performance were only very secondary considerations, and in military airships a high payload was important but in fact came to be subordinated to the need for the good speed and altitude performance of the type that was basically irrelevant to the civil airship. The LZ5 (the Imperial German Army's ZII of 1909) had a capacity of 530,000ft³ (15,000m³) and a length/beam ratio of 10.46/1 for its 446-ft (136-m) hull; the LZ18 (Imperial German Navy L2 of 1913) had a capacity of 953,500ft³ (27,000m³) and a length/beam ratio of 9.52/1 for its 518-ft (158-m) hull; the LZ40 (and naval L10 of 1915) had a capacity of 1,126,500ft³ (31,900 m³) and a length/beam ratio of 8.74/1 for its 536-ft (163-m) hull; the LZ62 (naval L30 of 1916) had a capacity of 1,949,000ft³ (55,200m³) and a length/beam ratio of 8.28/1 for its 649-ft (198-m) hull; and the LZ104 (naval L59 of 1917, and admittedly an 'odd man out' as it was built for a special purpose) had a capacity of 2,420,000ft³ (68,500m³) and a length/beam ratio of 9.48/1 for its 743-ft (226-m) hull. Then, after the end of the war the first new Zeppelin airship was the LZ120 Bodensee and this had a capacity of 785,750ft³ (22,250m³) and a length/beam ratio of 6.46/1 for its 396-ft

(120-m) hull. The implication of the LZ120's design was that the emphasis was no longer being placed so much on altitude and outright payload-carrying capability but rather on safety, comfort and general performance. However, the LZ126 built for the US Navy in 1924 had a capacity of 2,472,000ft³ (70,000m³) and a length/beam ratio of 6.27/1 for its 660-ft (200-m) hull; the LZ 127 Graf Zeppelin civil airship of 1928 had a capacity of 2,650,000ft³ (75,000m³) and a length/beam ratio of 7.76/1 for its 774-ft (236-m) hull; and the ultimate LZ129 Hindenburg civil airship of 1936 had a capacity of 7,000,000ft³ (198,000m³) and a length/beam ratio of 5.95/1 for its 800-ft (245-m) hull.

## LIFTING THE AIRSHIP

The hydrogen gas that provided the Zeppelin airships' lift was contained in the so-called *Traggaszellen* ('gas cells'). In the early airships these were made of a heavy cotton fabric covered with a rubber coating. Experience revealed that this combination was too porous to prevent gas escaping from the cells and pooling under the upper part of the outer covering, so the company

LEFT *One of the most important improvements in the Zeppelin airship's performance, especially in speed and range, was in the powerplant. The LZ1 was powered by the 14-hp (10-kW) Daimler engine.*

ABOVE *Greater capabilities were offered by the 170-hp (127-kW) Maybach engine, in a far better optimised installation with drive to a gearbox from which shafts (here not yet installed) extended upward and outward on each side to drive propellers.*

adopted a material that comprised two layers of cotton fabric with a heavier rubber coating. In 1908 the company experimented with goldbeater's skin attached to silk. Goldbeater's skin is the outer membrane of a cow's large intestine, and used by goldsmiths to facilitate the beating of gold into very thin layers. Trials revealed that while the material was very sensitive, it was also excellent for containing the gas and was therefore adopted in a form seven layers thick. During World War I supplies from Russia and the USA dried up, and the Zeppelin company had to use other materials, settling on an improved cotton after initial employment of silk.

The number of gas cells varied from class to class, the LZ1 having 17 and the number then oscillating slightly above and below this figure until a maximum of 19 cells was used in the LZ62 of 1916. The military and naval authorities generally preferred a larger number of cells in the belief that damage would not occur to all of the cells and therefore maximise the chances of a safe return to base, but the LZ59 had only 16 gas cells, and

the smaller Bodensee for civil use had a mere 12 gas cells. The volume of the gas cells was almost invariably 90 per cent of the hull's total volume, and features of each gas cell included an automatic pressure valve and also a manoeuvring valve controlled from the command position.

### ENGINE DESIGN

The Daimler N1899 four-cylinder inline engines used on the LZ1 each developed 14hp (10kW) at a weight of 850lb (385kg) for a power/weight ratio of 0.165 hp/lb (0.027kW/kg). Progress in the development of the piston engine was rapid during this period, and in the next few years the power of the Daimler engines was rapidly increased to 90hp (67kW), 100hp (75kW), 115hp (86kW) and finally 120hp (89kW) by 1910. Still greater power was needed, however, and a company was specially created to undertake the task of designing and building engines for Zeppelin airship use. This organisation was Karl Maybach's Maybach Motorenbau GmbH, whose first engine was the

LEFT *The 400-hp (298-kW) Maybach engine used in the LZ126 offered a higher power/weight ratio and was more reliable.*

RIGHT *The gondolas for the engines had to be light yet very strong, and were attached to the outside of the airship's main framework by sturdy struts.*

BELOW *The command gondolas of the Zeppelin airships in World War I had to be strong enough to carry the recoil forces of an increasingly potent defensive armament, in this instance a 20-mm cannon.*

Maybach A-Z six-cylinder inline unit of 1909 that was first used in the LZ9: this engine was rated at 145hp (108kW) and had a power/weight ratio of 0.146hp/lb (0.24kW/kg), and over the next few years formed the basis of a series of engines that were steadily increased in power output to 180hp (134kW) by 1913, 210hp (157kW) by 1914 and 240hp (179kW) by 1915. The naval airships, the LZ105 to LZ114 of the 'Type w' class (see Appendix) had H-S-Lu engines each rated at between 240 and 260hp (179 and 194kW), and offering a power/weight ratio of 0.28hp/lb (0.625kW/kg). Apart from their higher power and better power/weight ratios, another feature of the later engines was a specific fuel consumption only about half of that typical of the earlier engines.

A notable feature of these airship engines was the fact that they were designed for their specific application, and therefore included provision for fairly extensive maintenance and repair (including the changing of the valves and pistons) in flight by one of the mechanics included in the crew for this task. So successful were these Maybach engines that they were also used in Germany's other airships of the World War I period, namely those of the Gross-Basenach, Parseval and Schütte-Lanz companies. The skills of Maybach, who had originally designed engines for racing cars, were not limited to the engines he designed for airship use, and in 1916 he designed the excellent 245-hp (183-kW) MV.IV engine for aircraft use. For the LZ126, completed for service as the Los Angeles in 1924, Maybach produced the VL-1, a 12-cylinder

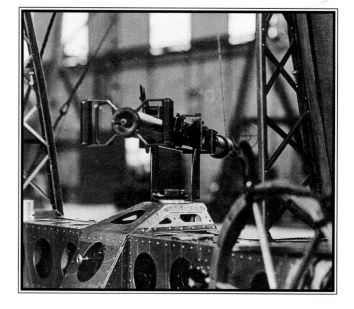

Vee engine rated at 400hp (298kW) for a weight of 2,070lb (940kg) and a power/weight ratio of 0.2hp/lb (0.32kW/kg) and also offering, despite its greater complexity and power, a further reduction in specific fuel consumption. This trend continued with VL-2 engines of the LZ127 Graf Zeppelin, which were each rated at 530hp (395kW), but in the LZ129 Hindenburg the powerplant was altered from five to four engines, although these 1,050-hp (783-kW) Daimler-Benz DB 602 Diesel engines were in fact designed by Maybach before its absorption into Daimler-Benz. The DB 602 was a

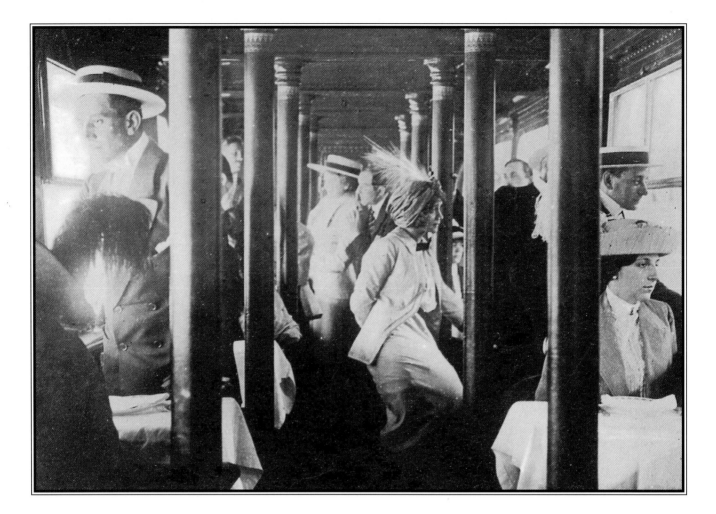

16-cylinder unit that weighed 4,170lb (1,890kg) and provided a power/weight ratio of 0.25hp/lb (0.41kW/kg).

The engines were installed in gondolas that were at first of simple yet sturdy design with a frame covered with fabric. Later gondolas were of Dural construction for greater strength in combination with lighter weight. In the LZ1 there were two engine gondolas, each carrying a single engine driving a propeller located high on the side of the hull. The first military airships had four engines installed as pairs in two gondolas, or three engines installed as a single unit at the rear of the forward gondola to drive a pusher propeller, and two in the rear gondola to drive propellers located high on the sides of the fuselage. This arrangement lasted to the advent of the LZ38 in the spring of 1915, and in this airship three of the four 180-hp (134-kW) Maybach C.X engines were installed in the rear gondola. To improve the general weight distribution of the airship, the arrangement that eventually became standard included two engines in the rear gondola to drive propellers located on the sides of the hull near its centre. Some later airship classes had a five- or six-engined powerplant, and the fastest of all the types, the 'Type x' class (see Appendix) typified by the LZ112 (naval L70 of summer 1918), had a seven-engined powerplant. In the final arrangement, adopted for a number of reasons including

ease of maintenance, the engines were fitted in large nacelles attached directly to the hull of the airship, and from here they drove the three-blade propellers by means of a shaft transmission arrangement. The Zeppelin company appreciated that the ideal arrangement, and one for which there was fully adequate volume, was inside the hull for the lowest possible drag, but this arrangement could not be adopted for safety reasons except in the American airships, which used helium rather than hydrogen as their lifting medium.

The fuel supply for the LZ1 was carried in each gondola together with the engine it supplied. From 1909 with the introduction of the LZ6, the fuel was carried in tanks inside the hull and supplied to the engines by a pressurised system and, in later airships, this was done by the use of gravity. The tanks were of aluminium alloy construction, and while the first units had a capacity of 22 imperial gallons (100 litres) the later tanks had a capacity of 88 imperial gallons (400 litres). The airships generally lifted off with 70 tanks of fuel for ordinary flights, but for its delivery flight across the Atlantic Ocean the LZ126 lifted off with 114 tanks of fuel. There was always oil storage to match the fuel capacity.

The propellers used by the Zeppelin airships were of many types. The LZ1 had small four-blade propellers very similar in

LEFT *Even in the early Zeppelin airships such as the Hansa, the passenger accommodation was comparatively spacious.*

RIGHT *Like other later Zeppelin airships, the LZ127, or Graf Zeppelin, featured considerably improved accommodation, including passenger cabins.*

BELOW *During the day, the passenger cabins on the LZ127 were converted to dayroom standard with the bed modified as a sofa.*

concept to the ship's propellers of the time, but between 1905 and 1908 three-blade propellers became standard, and later developments included a metal propeller with two paddle-like blades, then a similar unit with lengthened blades, and finally before World War I a four-blade propeller that gave way to another two-blade type.

This last type remained in production and use in airships until 1914, and was then steadily refined and strengthened for greater thrust and efficiency.

## PERFORMANCE

The payload/range performance of the early Zeppelin airships was very limited, but this was hardly surprising as they were more 'proof of concept' vehicles than airships designed to yield a real return on investment. By 1912 the average Zeppelin airship, typified by the LZ11 Viktoria Luise, had a lift of some 10,250lb (4,650kg), and by 1919 the LZ120 Bodensee had a lift of some 22,000lb (10,000kg). By comparison with these civil airships, which possessed a typical range of about 1,000

miles (1,700km), the military and naval airships provided greater lift and longer range, typically about 24,500lb (11,100kg) and 1,300 miles (2,100km) respectively. The demands of World War I then resulted in an enormous expansion of lift/range capability, and while the LZ40 (naval L10 of 1915) had a lift of 35,000lb (15,900kg) and possessed a range of 2,600 miles (4,200km), the comparative data for the LZ62 (naval L30 of 1916) were 61,700lb (28,000kg) and 4,600 miles (7,400km) and those for the LZ61 (naval L21 of 1916) were 99,200lb (44,500kg) and 7,455 miles (12,000km).

Between 1912 and 1914 the Viktoria Luise carried 9,738 service persons including crew and 2,995 fare-paying passengers, on 489 flights totalling 33,750 miles (54,310km) in 981 flying hours, while during the autumn of 1919 the Bodensee carried 4,050 persons including 2,253 fare-paying passengers on 103 trips totalling 31,851 miles (51,258km) in 532 flying hours. The later commercial airships of course had longer ranges, and the LZ127 could cover 6,370 miles (10,250km) and the LZ129 8,390 miles (13,500km). The lift of the LZ127 and LZ129 were 66,140lb and 132,275lb (30,000kg and 60,000kg) respectively.

ABOVE *The luxury of Zeppelin airship travel, here on the LZ127, was emphasised by the use of monogrammed silver and porcelain.*

LEFT *The dining saloon of the LZ127 offered comfortable accommodation, full waiter service, a good selection of wines, and the choice of hot or cold food from the galley or the cold table.*

dation, which now included a pilot's compartment, the radio operator's compartment, an officer's compartment and a position for a defensive machine-gun. The third of the gondola types was of a shorter length and introduced on the LZ95 (naval L48). On the LZ120 Bodensee intended for civil use, the gondola was considerably lengthened to the rear and now included a pilot's compartment and a passenger section with a lounge and other compartments.

Provision for the crew was altogether more austere, and comprised simple accommodation along the sides of the walkway inside the hull, where provision was made for hammocks to be slung. It was only with the advent of the ocean-crossing airships with their considerably longer endurance that more comfortable provision was made for the crew, who then enjoyed the benefits of sleeping cabins and common rooms.

Other features that came to be added to the standard equipment of Zeppelin airships included electric lighting by an engine-driven generator, and this first appeared in the LZ14 (naval L1) – earlier airships had relied on battery-powered lighting. Radio equipment was first used in the LZ6 (military ZIII), and the standard of flight and navigation equipment steadily improved, ranging from the compass and barometer of the LZ1 to the full suites of equipment typical of the LZ127 and LZ129.

Accommodation on the Zeppelin airships evolved from the very spartan open gondolas of the LZ1 to the luxurious fully enclosed spaces of the LZ127 and LZ129. The gondola of the LZ1 was large enough for the crew, engine and basic operational equipment. Over the following period there appeared three different types of gondola. The first of these, attached under the walkway, was a watertight assembly with a rounded front and a pointed rear. The second of these, which first made its appearance on the LZ36 (naval L9), was an enclosed control gondola about three times larger than it had been to provide accommo-

*The advanced military and naval airships set the pattern for the civil Zeppelin airships after the end of World War I, epitomised here by the LZ100 that had served as the naval L53.*

# CHAPTER FOUR

# Effects of War

By July 1914, the month before the outbreak of World War I, the Zeppelin commercial airships of the Delag organisation had carried a total of 34,038 passengers in the course of 1,582 flights, which had covered 113,420 miles (182,525km) in 3,175 flight hours. Three of the airships, namely the Deutschland I, Deutschland II and Schwaben, had been withdrawn from service and another three, namely the Viktoria Luise, Hansa and Sachsen, were still operational. The landing fields available to these airships at the time were those at Baden-Oos, Dresden, Düsseldorf, Frankfurt-am-Main, Hamburg and Leipzig.

Like the other airships of its 'Improved Schwaben' or 'Type h' class (see Appendix), the Sachsen, which had been manufactured during 1913, was some 460ft (140m) long with a maximum diameter of 49ft (15m) and a gas capacity of 688,600ft³ (19,500m³). The lifting gas was of course hydrogen, and this provided for a typical payload of 18,000lb (8,160kg). The transverse frames of the airship were divided almost evenly along the main length of the hull to create a cylindrical basic shape capped by tapered nose and tail sections. The frames themselves were of aluminium alloy construction with the 16 rubberised cotton gas cells between them, and there were two gondolas: the forward unit was the *Führergondel* (control car) containing the control section and an engine room, and the rear unit contained only an engine room. The gondolas were connected by a walkway, attached to the underside of the airship and looking like a triangular keel, and this carried the windowed passenger compartment. The four propellers were attached to outriggers high on

ABOVE *Tactical operations by army Zeppelins during World War I were hindered by the Allies' growing anti-aircraft capabilities, which included light field artillery and machine-guns on extemporised high-angle mountings.*

the hull of the airship in line with the gondolas, and were powered by three 180-hp (134-kW) Maybach B-Y six-cylinder engines for a maximum speed of 45mph (72km/h).

### AIRSHIPS AND THE ARMY

When World War I started in August 1914, the Imperial German Army impressed the three civilian airships and immediately started to convert them for military use. The process was basic in the extreme, and the main features of the effort were the removal of the wicker furniture from the passenger cabin so that the central walkway could be used for the carriage of bombs and the installation of a primitive bomb-aiming device. A partition was added to create a radio (or 'wireless' in the terminology of the day) room, and a single machine-gun was added in the forward gondola and the rear platform. The indicator letter Z, followed by a Roman numeral, replaced the airships' original civilian names: in this process the LZ22, LZ23 and LZ25 became the ZVII, ZVIII and ZIX respectively. These were not Imperial Germany's first Zeppelin airships, it should be added, for in 1909 it had taken delivery of the LZ3 and LZ5 as the ZI and ZII respectively; in 1911 the LZ9 had been taken on strength as the second airship named ZII; in 1912 the LZ12 had been

accepted as the ZIII; and in 1913 five other airships had been taken on strength as the LZ15, LZ16, LZ19, LZ20 and LZ21 became the second ZI, ZIV, third ZI, ZV and ZVI respectively.

At this time there was little to differentiate the new additions to the military fleet from their previous civilian airships created for the carriage of passengers and mail. The main changes were therefore in equipment and manning. These new military airships now had a crew of 19 men in the form of the commander, three other officers and 15 non-commissioned officers and men, bringing them into conformity with the other three Zeppelin airships already in military service. The airships designed specifically for military service by Zeppelin were in fact slightly larger than the commercial airships, having a volume of 803,100ft$^3$ (22,740 m$^3$), and the Imperial German Army also had one Schütte-Lanz airship that was based on the Eastern Front together with two of the Zeppelin airships for operations against the Russians. The other three airships were stationed near the Western Front to provide support for the German field armies operating against the Belgians, British and French.

### FIRST ASSIGNMENTS

The first military mission assigned to the airships was to drop bombs on strategic bridges and military objectives and to report troop movements. It was soon discovered, however, that the airships were too slow and limited in payload for effective use in this role, while their low cruising altitude combined with their poor speed made them comparatively simple targets for enemy gunners: as a result, three of the Zeppelin airships were lost quite soon.

The ZVI was ordered to provide support for the German right-wing attack on the Liége fortress system in Belgium during August 1914. However, after dropping three 110-lb (50-kg) bombs over a fort, the airship was forced to fly at a very low altitude and was repeatedly hit by small arms fire. The captain managed to keep his command in the air for some time, but then had to abandon the airship in a forest clearing near Bonn during the return flight to the base at Köln.

The ZVII was despatched to reconnoitre for the positions of French troops apparently falling back from the Elsass (Alsace) region after German forces had lost contact with them. But flying by night at an altitude of about 4,900ft (1,500m) from Baden-Oos towards the Vosges mountains, the Zeppelin's captain was strongly concerned that his airship might fly into one of the range's peaks, which average some 3,200ft (1,000m) and have a highest peak of 4,667ft (1,423m). The airship travelled through the night without incident, and during the morning found a force of French troops on which a number of small bombs were showered. A short distance further, the airship's crew discovered large concentrations of troops, and in an effort to secure more comprehensive information the captain ordered a descent to 2,790ft (850m). At once the air was full of exploding shells and small arms fire, and as the captain attempted to manoeuvre his airship away from this concentration of fire he presented the whole of the ZVII's side to the French, and suffered considerable damage during this necessarily slow turn. With many of its gas cells punctured, the ZVII could achieve little but a slowly descending crawl toward the safety of its base. However, it was unable to remain in the air and was wrecked near St Quirin in Lothringen (Lorraine).

The ZVIII lifted off during the same day from Trier, but this airship was peppered with small arms fire as it passed over a concentration of German troops, whose standards of 'aircraft recognition' clearly left much to be desired.

The unhappy crew little appreciated that this was merely a portent of things to come. The airship was only a few hundred feet in the air, and had still not unloaded its bombs, when quite suddenly it crossed over a force of Allied troops, on whom the bomb load was immediately dropped, the airship simultaneously being subjected to concentrated ground fire. With its control surfaces shot away and its gas cells punctured by innumerable bullets, the airship was unable to effect any meaningful escape and started to drop away downwind, losing height until it became

entangled in the trees of a wood near Badonviller. The crew attempted to fight off an approaching cavalry patrol, but then the captain ordered the crew to abandon the airship so that it could be set on fire to prevent it falling into the hands of the Allies. The airship had lost so much hydrogen gas that it was impossible to set an effective fire, however, and as they faded into the wood the crewmen saw the French cavalrymen hacking at the abandoned airship with their sabres. After 11 hours of stumbling through the wood, the surviving crewmen reached the German lines.

### BOMBING ATTACKS

With three airships lost in only a very short time, the German high command decided to step back, at least in the short term, from the concept of tactical operations by airship over land battlefields. Finally orders were issued that the Sachsen, which had replaced the lost ZVI at Köln, should bomb the important port of Antwerp that was still in Allied hands. The raid was successful, in that the airship returned to base unscathed after inflict-

BELOW *Even before the military and naval activities of World War I saw the rise and fall of Germany's Zeppelin airship force, the limited number of lighter-than-air craft suffered tragic losses. Seen here is the ZII that was destroyed near Weilburg in 1910.*

ing a little damage, but even now it was not altogether clear to the German high command that the airship was too large, too slow and too clumsy for commitment at low to medium altitudes over the land battlefield or well protected strategic targets. Orders were later issued for the ZIX to undertake bombing attacks on Antwerp, Calais, Dunkirk, Lille and Zeebrugge. By this time the standard bomb load had been increased to some 10 bombs, but the weight further degraded performance that was already too low and no significant results were achieved even though the airship did manage to survive. In the course of operations during the winter of 1914–15, the crews of the airships suffered very considerably from the weather as their craft lacked heating, and this was a further reason for the indifferent performance of the airships on longer-range missions and also for the steadily worsening morale of their crews.

During this period, the British also undertook very daring raids into German airspace to bomb the sheds in which the Zeppelin airships were based. The ZIX and LZ38 were lost at Düsseldorf and Brussels respectively, and the LZ37 was also destroyed, this time in the air.

Despite these losses, however, the number of airships available to the Imperial German Army climbed slowly but steadily as an expanded construction programme began to make its

effects felt. This was highly appreciated by the army where it was believed that the large rigid airship still had an important part to play in the land war, most specifically in the reconnaissance role. The expansion of the construction programme was made possible by the construction of a new factory at Potsdam and the expansion of the original facility at Friedrichshafen, where, by the end of World War I, there were eventually 1,600 technical staff and a workforce of 12,000. At this stage it was planned that Zeppelin would complete 26 airships for the Imperial German Army and Navy by 1915, and the programme was in fact so successful that Zeppelin was able to complete one new airship every 15 days with the aid of what was by now a production line system for the construction of standardised designs. These constituted a number of classes that had been steadily improved, one over the other, by the introduction of features to improve overall performance and reduce the limitations of earlier classes.

The ZXII (LZ26 of the 'Type n' class [see Appendix]) was completed in mid-December 1914 and had a gas volume of 883,000ft³ (25,000 m³) and could reach a maximum speed of 50mph (80km/h) with a powerplant of three 180-hp (134-kW) Maybach C-X engines: this was a significant improvement over the performance of the airship classes of the period before

LEFT *This scene of the landing of the Ersatz ZI ('Replacement ZI') was typical of the Zeppelin airship operations in winter, which could not have been comfortable for the many ground personnel.*

RIGHT *Above one of the Imperial German Navy's large Zeppelin airship sheds along Germany's North Sea coast, the LZ36 is seen here in 1915 in service as the L9.*

World War I, and other improvements included fully enclosed gondolas and the removal of part of the walkway inside the airship's outer covering. Poor features that were still retained included too great a length/beam ratio and the basically cylindrical shaping of the hull, although this latter did provide the advantage of allowing mass production of the hull frames for speed of manufacture and ease of replacement in damaged airships. Just as important as the higher speed, moreover, was the fact that the new classes of airship could reach somewhat greater altitudes than their predecessors, and this helped the airships (especially after they had dropped their bombs) to keep clear of the attentions of Allied aircraft.

### TARGET LONDON

A major shift in the basic nature of the airship war came when the German high command decided that the airships should start a bombing campaign against London and Paris, the capitals of their two main Western foes. This decision was taken only after the successful completion of many reconnaissance flights by Zeppelin airships over coastal areas and also a number of bombing missions against Antwerp and Ostend, which received about 9,920lb (4,500kg ) of bombs between them.

The airship chosen to make the first raid against London was the ZXII, and it set off on this epoch-making flight on 17 March 1915 under the command of Captain Ernst Lehmann. Nocturnal navigation was difficult at this time, especially from a control gondola under the hull of an airship, and once he had reached the southern edge of the North Sea, Lehmann plotted his course with reference to a lighthouse visible on the English side of the water barrier, which was covered by thick fog and provided only the occasional glimpse of England. For several hours the ZXII cruised above what Lehmann hoped was the English coastline in the hope of detecting the estuary of the River Thames, up which he then hoped to fly. No landmark was seen, however, even after the crew of the airship had lowered one of their number in a basket that had still not penetrated the fog at the end of its line. Lehmann now conceded defeat and ordered a return to base via Calais.

The fog closed in round the Zeppelin as it approached the French coast, and Lehmann ordered the engines to be reduced to minimum speed to quieten the airship as it cruised over the French port. The basket was again lowered, and this time the observer was able to direct the Zeppelin over the fortifications of the port, allowing them to be bombed accurately. The ZXII remained over Calais for some three-quarters of an hour, dropping its bombs singly and only after the most careful approach to the intended target. It then departed at 4,900ft (1,500m) for base after all the bombs had been dropped.

Fog was also encountered over the landing field, so the ZXII made a dead-reckoning approach with compass and altimeter, although a fall in pressure since the airship's lift-off meant that the ZXII landed slightly inaccurately on a nearby railway, and was moved into its hangar the following morning for some two weeks of repairs. The ZXII's second attempt to reach London was no more successful, in this instance as a result of rain rather than fog, and again Lehmann decided to bomb a secondary target on his way back to base. The target this time was Dunkirk, where again the fortifications were bombed, but in the absence

of cloud or fog the huge airship was seen by the troops on the ground, who peppered the ZXII with fire and caused some damage including the loss of a complete propeller. Even so, the airship reached its base for a further bout of repairs. The third attempt to bomb London was also a failure, and the ZXII bombed Harwich on the English coast before returning to base.

### TARGET PARIS

Greater success attended the Germans' early efforts to use airships for attacks on targets in continental Europe. Here the most important single target was Paris, which was doubly attractive as it was not only the capital of France but, unlike London, it could be approached and identified easily as the French were unwilling to impose any real blackout. The German efforts against Paris were also aided by the generally more clement nature of the weather.

The three airships ordered into action for the first raid against Paris on 21 March 1915 were the ZX, LZ35 and SLII, the last of these a Schütte-Lanz machine. Navigation toward Paris by night was aided by the specially arranged coded flashes from searchlights at Douai, Cambrai, Noyon and other points on the airships' path. As a result, the attackers found Paris without difficulty, but by this time their number had been reduced

ABOVE *The LZ36 was completed for a first flight on 8 March 1915 and survived to 16 September 1916, when it was destroyed in its hangar as an adjacent airship, the LZ31 (L6), caught fire.*

to two Zeppelin airships after the SLII had been damaged by shell fire over the front line and forced back to base, although only after dropping its bombs on what its commander hoped was the Allied headquarters at Compiègne.

Under the command of Captain Horn, the ZX overflew Paris at 8,200ft (2,500m), well above the effective reach of the anti-aircraft artillery batteries, and was therefore able to cruise over the city for about 30 minutes as the captain selected the targets (including an electricity-generating station and a factory) for accurate bombing. The French had meanwhile worked out the airship's likely course and set a trap near Noyon, where French guns hit the airship as it was cruising at 9,850ft (2,950m) and punctured five of its gas cells. It was only by dint of casting overboard just about anything that could be shifted that the airship was able to remain airborne long enough to reach a safe haven at St Quentin.

Under the command of Captain Masius, the LZ35 also bombed targets in Paris with considerable accuracy, but was caught by the searchlights of a motorised anti-aircraft unit, which tracked the airship for some distance as it headed back to base. It managed to dodge the French unit and reached safety without undue damage.

### THE EASTERN FRONT

The three airships based behind the Eastern Front at the beginning of the war were the SLII, the ZIV and the ZV, the latter two commanded respectively by Captain Quast and Captain Grüner. The SLII was initially used to support the Austro-Hungarian army on the southwestern sector of the Eastern Front, but was soon posted to the Western Front. The ZIV bombed strategically important targets such as the railway junctions and marshalling yards near Warsaw and other major cities, but was withdrawn from operational service and used only as a training airship after being riddled with small arms fire during a low-level sortie. The ZV undertook a number of successful reconnaissance flights before being forced down at the end of August 1914 after it was hit by Russian artillery fire while bombing the marshalling yards at Mlawa, and its crew captured.

The two Zeppelin airships on the Eastern Front were replaced by another two Zeppelin machines, in this instance the ZXI and LZ34. Both the vessels were lost on the same day in May 1915, the ZXI as a result of storm damage in its hangar and the LZ34 after being hit in the air by Russian artillery fire. The replacements for the two airships were the ZXII and LZ39, later augmented by the LZ79 and LZ85 to provide the Germans with a more significant capability in the bombing campaign against the marshalling yards and railway junctions that the Russians used with considerable success to shift their forces around the Eastern Front.

During 1915, the Imperial German Army ordered several other airships to the Eastern Front after the Western Front had become too dangerous for them. The Zeppelin airships had a new but short period of success on the Eastern Front and also in associated regions such as the Balkans, but when the loss rate in the East began to approach that which had earlier been reached in the West, the army decided to pull out of airship operations and handed over its surviving machines to the navy.

Before this development, however, in February 1916 the army had seven new airships. The LZ90 and her sisters had a gas volume of 1,130,000ft³ (32,000m³) and were constructed in a more streamlined teardrop shape, with a tapered stern and more efficient controls. Other features of the design were a defensive armament of up to eight machine-guns (two in each of the three gondolas and single guns on the upper platform and in the stern) and the powerplant of four 240-hp (179-kW) H-S-Lu engines for a cruising altitude of 9,800ft (3,000m) and a bomb load of 6,600lb (3,000kg), increasing to 12,000ft (3,600m) without bombs. However, hand-in-hand with the improvement in Zeppelin airship capabilities as typified by the LZ90 went the enhancement of the Allied powers' ability to tackle these airships, including incendiary ammunition to puncture the airship's gas cells and then ignite the mix of hydrogen and air thus created (the LZ77 was the first victim of the new type of ammunition), aircraft whose performance increased more rapidly than

BELOW *Notable on the LZ43 (in service as the naval L12) is a position on the forward hull for a 7.92-mm (0.312-in) MG 08 machine-gun, evidence of the growing ability of Allied fighters to intercept and shoot down Zeppelin airships.*

that of the airships, networks of barrage balloons, and the development of anti-aircraft guns with a higher effective ceiling and greater muzzle velocity.

## COMPETITION

In overall terms, therefore, the army decided that the pace of technological development meant that the heavier-than-air craft now had an unassailable superiority over the lighter-than-air craft, at least of the free-flying type, and as a result the airship had ceased to be an asset. This was all the more evident as heavier-than-air technology was now opening the way for heavier-than-air bombers able to carry a warload equal to that of the Zeppelin airships at a higher speed, albeit over a shorter range. After a final raid by the LZ107 on Boulogne on 16 February 1917, the army ordered that its airship operations would cease forthwith. With the exception of four units transferred to the navy for patrols over the Baltic Sea, all the army's existing airships were reduced to produce.

Before abandoning the airship, the Imperial German Army had operated 33 Zeppelin airships, and an overall total of 50 airships, since the outbreak of war, and these had achieved a total of 232 operational sorties. Their reconnaissance work, especially over the larger and less heavily armed regions typical of Eastern Front operations, had generally been of great success, and in the course of 111 raids the airships had delivered some 132,700lb (60,000kg) of bombs over Russian targets, 98,300lb (44,600kg) of bombs over French targets, 80,500lb (36,500kg) of bombs over English targets within an overall bomb weight of 311,500lb (141,100kg). Of the service's total of 50 airships, 17

had been lost to enemy action and two to anti-aircraft fire, while eight had been wrecked as a result of other causes. The service's dead comprised 15 officers and 50 other ranks.

## THE NAVY STEPS IN

The other significant operator of the Zeppelin airship in World War I, and indeed the more important of the two services in terms of the size and ambitions of its airship operations, was the Imperial German Navy, which had taken delivery of its first Zeppelin airship in 1912. This was the LZ14, which was designated as the L1 in naval service. The L1 was slightly larger than contemporary army airships and had been specially designed for safe operation under the more adverse weather conditions typical of naval operations. Since the navy had no hangar of its own, the L1 used the open harbour at Hamburg for temporary mooring.

Von Zeppelin himself had commanded the L1 in October on its delivery flight from Friedrichshafen to Berlin, and in the course of this flight cruised over the North Sea, passing over the edge of Denmark before making for Berlin. The navy was very happy with the success of this flight, which had covered a distance of over 1,000 miles (1,600km) and had lasted some 31 hours. After a mere six months of service, however, the airship went down in the sea: caught in a severe storm off the coast of Heligoland on 9 September 1913, the L1 came down and was totally wrecked after crashing into the sea. Of the 32 men on board, only six were saved.

Despite this loss, the navy immediately contracted for another airship. The L2 (LZ18) was to be both larger and stronger, and fitted with a powerplant of four 180-hp (134-kW) Maybach

LEFT *During World War I, the Zeppelin airship force played an important long-range scouting role for the navy's High Seas Fleet. The unit seen here is the LZ41 in service as the L11.*

RIGHT *Although still based on an essentially cylindrical central hull section, the LZ43, in service as the L12, had longer and more finely tapered bow and stern sections giving the airship a generally finer line.*

C-X engines. A third gondola was added to serve as the bridge car, and for extra protection against the elements this was enclosed with a type of celluloid material. All three gondolas were connected by a walkway inside the lower part of the hull.

On its delivery flight to Berlin on 17 October 1913, the L2 performed well, but when taking off after being handed over to the navy, it caught fire and crashed. All of the crew were killed.

The L3 entered naval service in May 1914. This was actually the LZ24, which had been named Hansa in civil service, that was taken over from the Delag and initially despatched to Dresden as part of its naval 'shake-down' cruise. By this time the navy had decided that the Zeppelin airship could be a useful adjunct in its efforts to become a blue-water rather than just coastal-defence navy, and by the end of the year had two more Zeppelin airships in service, one of them for use as a training ship.

The L3 made a total of 141 reconnaissance flights over the North Sea, including one that lasted as long as 34 hours. Soon after the outbreak of World War I the navy also acquired the L4 and L5, and by the end of 1914 one of these had flown some 50 reconnaissance flights over the Baltic Sea. The navy then acquired a batch of three Zeppelin airships, namely the L6, L7 and L8. The problem at this time was that the navy was effectively out of trained airship crew, and as a result the L6 was allocated to a relatively inexperienced officer, Lieutenant Horst Freiherr Treusch von Buttlar-Brandenfels, and officers of similarly low rank received command of the other two airships.

These early Zeppelin airships, converted from commercial airships, could lift only three 110-lb (50-kg) bombs carried in what was originally the passenger cabin in the centre of the walkway between the two gondolas. When the airship was over its target, the gunnery officer cut the ropes that held the bomb in place.

On its first patrol over the North Sea, the L6 was hit by small-arms fire from a mine-laying vessel and suffered some 600 holes in its gas cells, causing difficulties in effective control of the airship. Odd though it may sound, given the highly inflammable nature of hydrogen, such punctures were not too dangerous, however, for the bullet tended to pass right through the airship and it was only from the upper hole that hydrogen was lost. When the proper ventilation had been provided, this would emerge from the top of the envelope and dissipate into the outside air before there was any chance of ignition.

## NAVAL AIRSHIPS ENGAGED

The navy's first large-scale contact with the British Royal Navy took place on 15 December after British warships had been reported near Heligoland. The L5 and L6 were instructed to fly a reconnaissance of the area, and in the process sighted several British seaplanes apparently involved on a raid to the Nordholz base. Because of their faster speed, the aircraft were able to evade the airships when the latter tried to intercept. The L5 headed for the carrier from which the seaplanes had been launched, and discovered two seaplanes on the water near the carrier. The airship used machine-gun fire and small bombs to destroy the seaplanes.

The other airship, the L6, sighted some 20 mine-layers on its return flight, but its radio equipment failed and the airship was therefore unable to call in the German surface forces that might have crushed the force of British ships. The mine-layers were soon joined by their two protecting cruisers, the *Arethusa* and the *Undaunted*, as well as some destroyers. Small-arms fire greeted the Zeppelin airship as it cruised above the warships, but machine-gun fire from the Zeppelin then speedily cleared the decks of the warships. However, as the airship was manoeuvring for a bombing attack, a German seaplane intervened and dropped two bombs that missed the warship. The Zeppelin's bombs also missed.

During 1915 the airships of the Imperial German Navy flew some 389 long-range reconnaissance missions and participated in 30 raids on England. Initially the airships were used in a somewhat haphazard fashion, but after several months the Zeppelin airship raids on England began to develop a specific and definite tactic, with the only variable factor the number of airships employed. Any Zeppelin airship involved in a raid departed from its base as close to 12.00 a.m. as was possible and, after loitering, made rendezvous with the other airships lifting off from the same base, making a loose formation and cruising at an altitude of only a few hundred feet over the Heligoland Bight. Here the groups of airships from the Alhorn, Hage, Nordholz, Tondern and Wittmundhaven bases made rendezvous with each other but thereafter did not fly in any type of close formation. As the airships approached the east coast of England, each commander tried to discover a point at which his airship could cross the coast without detection during the dark of the night that now covered the attacking force.

Typical of the early raids on England was the attack planned for 18 January 1915. The airships allocated to the operation were the L3, L4, L5 and L6, but the only two to reach their targets and make their attacks were the L3 and L4 under the command of Lieutenant Commanders Hans Fritz and Magnus Graf von Platen-Hallermund respectively. Navigation was difficult, as all the British landmarks were blacked-out, but the beams of the lighthouses at Ostend and Steenbrugge formed an imaginary line pointing directly to the mouth of the River Thames, whose shining reflection led to London. The other ships experienced troubles of various kinds and were forced to return to their bases at Nordholz. Another attack was made, under suitable weather conditions, during April. But by then the L3 and the L4 had been lost in a storm.

The base at Nordholz was soon increased in size and capability to cater for the increasing numbers of airships and their larger crews. Other airships were added to the fleet, but because of serious losses, the number of Zeppelin airships actually in ser-

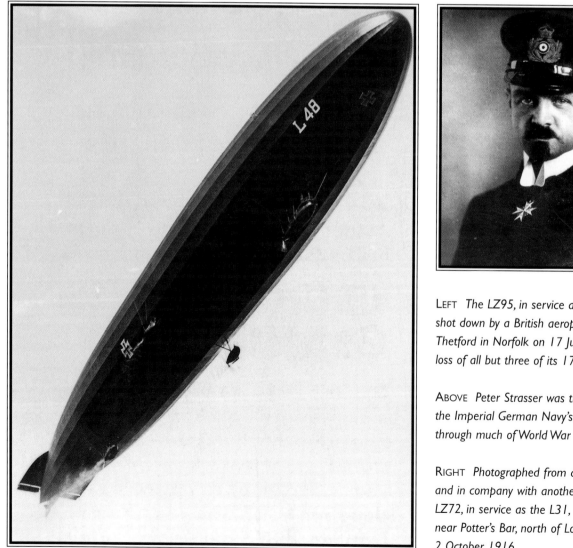

LEFT *The LZ95, in service as the L48, was shot down by a British aeroplane near Thetford in Norfolk on 17 June 1917 with the loss of all but three of its 17-man crew.*

ABOVE *Peter Strasser was the commander of the Imperial German Navy's airship division through much of World War I.*

RIGHT *Photographed from a Zeppelin airship and in company with another two airships, the LZ72, in service as the L31, was shot down near Potter's Bar, north of London, on 2 October 1916.*

vice at any one time increased only slowly. The L8 was lost in March 1915 while returning from a raid on the English coast. With its gas cells perforated by artillery shells, the disabled ship came down in Belgium and was destroyed by a storm. The L7 also suffered a similar fate: after escaping an initial naval interception and possible destruction when it passed over a flotilla at low altitude, the airship passed over a second naval force and was hit and damaged so badly that it came down in the sea near Horns Reef on the Danish coast, where it was shelled and destroyed by the deck gun of an Allied submarine that surfaced to accomplish the task.

After dropping its bombs, the L6 made a low-altitude run over some British destroyers for a machine-gun attack, but took a large number of hits from the ships and only just managed to reach it base at Nordholz, where it was lost to fire as it tried to land. The L9 also burned, this time while being filled with hydrogen. The L9, it should be noted, was the first of the larger 'Type o' class of Zeppelin airship (see Appendix), and under the command of Lieutenant Commander Heinrich Mathy had been successful in sinking a submarine off Terschelling on 3 May 1915. The L10 was later struck by lightning over its base in September 1915 while venting hydrogen. It was completely destroyed.

However, what the naval airships did best was maritime reconnaissance, and in this role their performance was excellent. To quote but one instance, during its return flight from a raid, the L19 spotted three British warships carrying aircraft for an attack on the German mainland. The Zeppelin airship then dropped one bomb from high altitude, hitting one of the ships that had already lowered one of its seaplanes into the water in preparation for take-off for the bombing raid, and also used its radio to alert German warships in the area, thereby preventing the planned air raid.

Early operations against England soon persuaded the Imperial German Navy that the early classes of Zeppelin airships were too small for their task. Although they had moderate range and endurance, they could only travel at a relatively low speed and at a poor cruising altitude, and could also carry only a very modest bomb load. Superior capabilities were offered by the 'Type q' and 'Type r' classes of airships (see Appendix) that entered service with designations between L20 and L41, but the better performance of these airships was offset by the greater defence capabilities that the British had developed and could now bring to bear against them.

On one raid, a Zeppelin airship under the command of Lieutenant Commander Horst Freiherr Treusch von Buttlar-Brandenfels was hit by ground-fire and suffered major damage to its central gas cells, causing the airship to become unbalanced and unable to maintain height. As the airship's captain was working out where to land on the sea, loud cracking noises indicated that the ship was about to break in two. Hans von Schiller, the executive officer and a man known for his quick wit, asked his captain if he wished to command the bow or the stern portion

ABOVE *The LZ104, built for navy service as the L59, became the remarkable Afrikaschiff ('Africa ship') that flew an extraordinary mission deep into Africa in a vain effort to deliver supplies to the German forces there.*

after the break-up, so that he himself could then take charge of the other part. But the expected break never actually occurred. Flying slowly at an altitude of 3,200ft (1,000m), the crew hoped to stay aloft until after sunrise when, with some luck, the warmth of the shining sun would cause the remaining gas to expand sufficiently to keep the crippled airship in the air long enough to reach land, and this is in fact what happened.

By the start of 1916 all airships were ordered to carry parachutes so the members of the crew would have at least a chance to save themselves if their craft caught fire. But it was difficult to find effective but accessible storage space for these bulky and weighty items, whose carriage reduced the weight of fuel or bombs that could be lifted by 2,205lb (1,000kg). Most crews elected not to carry parachutes, and these were later officially designated as optional rather than mandatory items of equipment.

The airships of the Imperial German Navy were also used on occasion for tasks other than bombing and patrolling. For instance, when a storm devastated a number of the small islands off the German coast, the L16 carried provisions to the inhabitants of these North Sea islands, isolated by raging seas. Landing successfully on each of the islands, the airship brought much needed relief to the stricken people. On another occasion the L23 was launched to search for a downed flying boat. The drifting machine was located and its crew was taken on board,

but it was only after salvaging the flying boat's engine that the Zeppelin airship then returned to base. Later, the same airship, under the command of Lieutenant Commander Ludwig Bockholt, discovered an unidentified schooner in a prohibited area and went down to investigate. After a small bomb had been dropped in front of her bow, the vessel duly stopped her engines, and the Zeppelin airship landed on the calm sea behind her and the captain sent a small party to board the schooner, which was discovered to be carrying contraband goods and then ordered by Bockholt to sail for Cuxhaven. A tender was called by radio to take possession of this prize, and pending the arrival of the tender the Zeppelin airship remained over the captured vessel.

### DEFENCE MEASURES

By September 1916, the British military authorities had vastly improved their system of air defences over London, and also started to employ high-performance aircraft as interceptors. The Zeppelin airships' only practical defence against these aircraft was to climb above them, and it was discovered that an altitude of 13,125ft (4,000m) was generally sufficient for immunity against interception. Throughout most of World War I the advantage generally remained with the airships in this regard, although improvements at times benefited one side or the other. Another advantage enjoyed by the Zeppelin airship was its considerably greater endurance, which generally allowed it to outlast or outrange its opponents.

Even so, there were major losses. During one of their night attacks on England, the force of Zeppelin airships was caught in very adverse weather and then thick fog. The L34 was shot down over Hartlepool, the L21 was shot down near the east coast at Yarmouth, and the L36 crashed near its base. The L39, on the return from England, was driven over the French headquarters at Compiègne, where it was lost to concentrated antiaircraft fire. The L22 and the L43 were lost over the North Sea, and the L48 was shot down over England. It had been a disastrous raid for the seven participating airships.

On 2 September 1916 some 13 airships were launched on a raid against London. The SLII, a Schütte-Lanz airship, was soon shot down in flames, and as a result the German high command ordered that airships should fly at an altitude of at least 14,800ft (4,400m) and, it was hoped, 17,200ft (5,150m) over the heavily protected British capital. Since none of the Zeppelin airships currently in service could reach that altitude, no further attacks on London were ordered until a new generation of improved airship could be designed, manufactured and placed in service.

A major attack on England was planned for 19 October 1917, when some 13 airships were instructed to raid the indus-

trial cities of Sheffield and Manchester as well as the port of Liverpool. The raid got off to a poor start as neither the L42 nor the L51 were able to leave the Alhorn base because of strong cross-winds. The 11 airships which started were the L1, L44, L45, L46, L47, L49, L50, L52, L53, L54 and L55. When the weather deteriorated, some of the captains flew farther to the north than originally planned, but others in fact reached the south coast of England. One of the Zeppelin airships drifted so far south that instead of flying over Sheffield, the commander discovered that he was actually over London. At the airships' designated altitude of 16,400ft (5,000m), a combination of storm and cloud made matters so difficult that some of the airships were forced to climb to 21,000ft (6,300m), their very maximum altitude. After several hours of suffering in the cold and thin air at this altitude, the airships tried to reach the

BELOW *The Zeppelin raids on London did not inflict massive physical damage or very high civilian casualties, but the moral shock of the campaign was enormous.*

ABOVE *The control gondola of the LZ86 had the conning position in its forward section, two lateral positions for machine-guns in the centre, and a rear engine to drive a pusher propeller.*

European coast to which they were closest, and then make their way back to base.

Disaster awaited, however. Four of the Zeppelin airships drifted over France, unable to escape the strong winds, and were shot down over hostile territory when they were forced down to a lower altitude. The L44 was brought down near Lunéville. The other three were still over enemy territory as they ran out of fuel: the L45 landed in the valley of the Durance river and its crew set the ship on fire; the L49 also landed and its crew was captured; as the crew of the L50 started to disembark after an emergency landing, the ship suddenly lifted off the ground and was carried by the strong wind into the higher mountains of Switzerland. Here, the rest of the crew got out of the airship safely, which rose once again into the air and disappeared never to be found. The men who had landed died at this spot, and their frozen bodies were discovered later. A fifth Zeppelin airship, the L55, was attacked by aircraft over France, but climbed by jettisoning all weight and even some fuel: at a height of 25,000ft (7,500m), blood started to run from the noses, mouths and ears of the men, the water supply turned to ice, and despite being laced with alcohol the engines' cooling water froze. The Zeppelin airship was unable to reach its base at Alhorn and was forced to land at Tiefenrot on the Werra river,

where it was dismantled. The October attack had been a complete disaster, that resulted in the loss of five new Zeppelin airships together with their invaluable crews.

## DELIVERY TO AFRICA

In August 1917 Zeppelin introduced the 'Type v' class airship (see Appendix) intended for naval reconnaissance and bombing roles. For more than a year this remained the 'standard' airship of the navy's airship division. At much the same time, small German forces in East Africa, under the command of General Paul von Lettow-Vorbeck, were fighting a highly successful campaign that was tying down very substantial numbers of Allied troops. These German forces had no source of supplies other than what they could capture from the Allies, however, and were rapidly exhausting their stocks of German weapons and ammunition. This army, which had recently abandoned all its lighter-than-air capability, therefore asked the navy for assistance in delivering supplies and equipment to East Africa. Given the implications of von Lettow-Vorbeck's successes for Germany's international prestige and also for national morale, the navy acceded to the request, and ordered from Zeppelin a development of the 'Type v' class airship (see Appendix) with the ability to deliver a useful payload from Jamboli in Bulgaria, the most southeasterly base held by the European members of the Central Powers, to Mahenge in southern Tanganyika (now Tanzania). This was a distance of some 3,600 miles (5,800km) that would have to be covered without any intermediate stops and in a flight time of four or five days depending on ambient wind direction and speed.

The demand was for a payload of some 35,800lb (16,200kg) delivered over the full range, and the early calculations of the Zeppelin design team indicated that a gas volume of 2,366,000ft³ (67,000m³) would be required for the movement of such a payload together with the fuel needed for the range. The army had already advised von Lettow-Vorbeck by intermittent and not altogether reliable radio that the delivery would be made during October, and as this left inadequate time for the design and construction of an all-new airship with this gas volume, Zeppelin was forced to undertake a development of the 'Type v' class design (see Appendix) in an effort to meet both the requirement and the schedule.

This resulted in the development of two 'Type w' class airships (see Appendix). This was in essence the incomplete hull of a 'Type v' class airship lengthened to accommodate two additional gas cells, each 49ft (15m) long. The airship was completed with the same company designation, LZ102, and made its maiden flight toward the end of September 1917 before being accepted for navy service with the designation L57. The airship was wrecked and burned in a storm off Jütebog on 8 October of the same year, however, and despite the fact that as captain he had been at least partially responsible for the accident, to avoid the delays that would have resulted from the appointment of a new captain, Ludwig Bockholt was appointed to command the LZ104 (L59) that was immediately ordered as a replacement.

Because of the strong sun and general heat likely to be encountered over Africa, the L59 was completed without the usual black protective coating, which in addition to its weight could have caused a major overheating of the hydrogen in the gas cells. It had also been taken into account that the airship would not return to Europe, but that the unpainted fabric covering of the hull would be turned to many uses, such as tents and packs, in East Africa.

On the morning of 3 November 1917, the L59 left the Zeppelin factory at Staaken, near Berlin, where it had been built and headed for Jamboli. The airship carried in its hold a large assortment of munitions as well as 30 machine-guns with spare parts, 61 bags of medical supplies, a large quantity of mail, and various tropical outfits. From Jamboli, Bockholt made two unsuccessful attempts to reach East Africa, where the German colonial forces were reaching ever more desperate straits. They could no longer stand their ground against the British, who had received information of the impending arrival of the L59 and had determined to seize the area in which it expected to find German ground forces as it arrived. On 21 November the airship made a third attempt at getting through to East Africa, unaware of the fact that von Lettow-Vorbeck had been forced to

BELOW *Airship stations, such as the Zeppelin facility at Staaken, north Germany (photographed in 1918), were typified by a large landing area, vast hangars, personnel quarters, an administrative centre and a gas-generation plant.*

ABOVE *The command gondola of Zeppelin airships was carried below the forward part of the hull by sturdy struts.*

RIGHT *Interior view of the conning position of the LZ104, in service as the naval L59.*

surrender the day before. The German high command tried to recall the L59 using the powerful radio transmitter at Nauen near Berlin, but could not get through to Bockholt's crew.

The airship meanwhile crossed Turkey and by evening was crossing the eastern tip of Crete, where an imminent thunderstorm made radio reception impossible. Early in the morning of the following day, the L59 reached the coast of North Africa near Mersa Matruh, and the German airship now faced the prospect of crossing the long stretch of barren Libyan desert. The heat of the sun soon heated the gas cells, and the valves in each automatically released hydrogen to avoid the possibility of too high a pressure in the cells. The hull became extremely dry, and the airship rolled and pitched as it continued south, and then southeast, in an increasing nose-heavy condition. In the middle of the afternoon the L59 flew over the palm groves of the Dakhla oasis, with everything still functioning properly.

One hour later, however, one of the five engines broke down and, as bad luck would have it, this was the engine that drove the electrical generator powering the radio equipment. The engine could not be repaired, but Bockholt decided to press on, nursing the four surviving engines to try to prevent any of them from breaking down as a result of over-active employment. Late in the evening, the L59 reached the River Nile at Wadi Halfa

and turned south along the western bank. With the evaporation of the day's heat, however, the airship was now becoming increasingly heavy as a result of the day's loss of hydrogen, and the task of maintaining a trim became increasingly arduous.

Shortly past midnight, one of the many recall signals broadcast from Nauen was finally received in the airship, and Bockholt finally turned back at a point to the northwest of Khartoum. The long return flight took until 25 November, when the L59 reached Jamboli after 95 hours in the air since its departure. Under the most difficult of operating conditions, the L59 had covered a distance of 4,000 miles (6,500km), and still had fuel for another 64 hours of flight, although all 22 members of the crew were utterly exhausted. Even though the L59 did not succeed in the object of its flight, this was nonetheless one of the greatest achievements in airship history.

### BACK TO BATTLE

There followed considerable controversy, which included even Kaiser Wilhelm II, about the purpose to which the L59 should now be put. Lieutenant Commander Peter Strasser, head of the Imperial German Navy's airship division, wanted to have the airship flown back to Germany for use in the reconnaissance role, but Bockholt ignored the chain of command and suggested directly to the naval staff that the L59 should remain at Jamboli and be used for attacks on Allied targets in Italy and the Middle East. Wilhelm II was instrumental in the decision going in Bockholt's favour, and in January 1918 the airship returned to Germany for the necessary modifications.

The L59 returned to Jamboli on 21 February 1918, and on 10 March attacked the naval base and a number of factories in the Naples area with 14,000lb (6,300kg) of bombs released from an altitude of 11,800ft (3,500m). An attack on Port Said planned for 20 March could not be effected, however, as the airship encountered a strong headwind. This happened again during an attempt to bomb the British naval base in the Bay of Soudha in Crete.

The L59 lifted off from Jamboli for the last time on 7 April 1918 with the British bastion of Malta as its objective. The airship crossed the Balkans and then the Strait of Otranto, and here, during the evening, the crew of the German submarine U-53 saw a few flashes of light and then a mass of flame that lit up the whole horizon. Shortly after this an explosion echoed through the strait. The L59 had finally met its end on its 17th naval flight, presumably as a result of an on-board accident that ignited the hydrogen gas and then set off the bomb load.

The airship base at Alhorn had consisted of six hangars when, in January 1918, the L51 caught fire from some undetermined cause while inside one of the hangars. The fire spread with amazing rapidity to the other four airships, namely the

ABOVE *At the technical level, the civil airship Bodensee, completed in 1919, was in essence a shortened civilian version of the naval airships built in the latter part of World War I.*

L46, L47, L58 and SL20. All were destroyed. Exhaustive investigations were made as to the cause of this mysterious holocaust, but no definitive conclusions were reached. Some airship bases were also bombed by the British: Tondern was attacked in July 1918, resulting in the destruction of the L54 and the L60 as they lay in their hangars.

The last raid against England was carried out on 9 August 1918 by five of the 'Type v' and 'Type x' airships under the command of Strasser. As *Führer der Luftschiffe* ('Chief of Airships'), who had first seen active service on the Sachsen, Strasser now seldom had an opportunity to fly and saw the opportunity to take to the air in the latest and most advanced type Zeppelin airship as a heaven-sent chance.

The four 'Type v' class airships had a capacity of 2,189,500ft³ (62,000m³) while the 'Type x' class L71 had a capacity of 2,419,000ft³ (68,500m³) and were powered by five or seven 245-hp (183-kW) Maybach MB.IVa supercharged engines. On the L71 one of the engines was placed in the front gondola, two in the rear gondola, and one each in the four lateral gondolas, giving this Zeppelin airship an average speed of about 73mph (117km/h). The airships could also climb to an altitude of 25,300ft (7,700m), and thus regained their superiority over current Allied aircraft.

By this time, it should be noted, plans were being made for the construction of a whole new series of Zeppelin airships to a design with a capacity of 2,650,000ft³ (75,000m³) and a maximum speed of 90mph (145km/h). The planned LZ100 was to be even larger than the others and to possess protection against incendiary bullets. But the last of the 88 Zeppelin airships produced for the military services, the LZ113, was the last of the special *Kriegsluftschiffe* ('war airships'). It marked a very significant advance over the earliest type: with a capacity of 2,419,000ft³ (68,500m³). It had a powerplant producing an overall total of 2,030hp (1,514kW) for a maximum speed of 80mph (130km/h) and a ceiling of 26,200ft (7,800m), with a total lift of 114,600lb (52,000kg).

Strasser, knowing that the era of the military airship was drawing to a close, at least as far as bombing operations were concerned, wanted to cap his career with something of a milestone, and took part in the mission on board the L70 under the command of Lieutenant Commander Johann von Lossnitzer. However, the cold weather prevented the airship from rising above 17,300ft (5,200m) and it was at this altitude that the Zeppelin airship was shot down, with the loss of all on board, by a British warplane before it had even reached the English coast.

During World War I, the Imperial German Navy operated 78 airships. Of these, nine were of the Schütte-Lanz rigid type, three were of the Parseval non-rigid type and one was a Gross-Badenach semi-rigid type. The total of Zeppelin airships was 65, of which six were operated only for training. The airship

ABOVE *British troops guard the wreckage of the LZ74 (naval L32), shot down by a British aeroplane near Great Burstead on 24 September 1916.*

RIGHT *The salient features of the naval Zeppelin airships built in World War I are shown in this chart, giving an indication of the increasing size and better streamlining as the war progressed.*

| Marine-Luftschiffe | | Länge in m | Inhalt in cbm | Nutzlast in kg | Geschw. m/sec | Steighöhe in m | Baujahr |
|---|---|---|---|---|---|---|---|
| L 3 — 8 | | 158 | 22470 | 9200 | 23,4 | 2500 | 1914/15 |
| L 9 | | 161,4 | 24900 | 11000 | 23,6 | 3000 | 1915 |
| L 10 — 19 | | 163,5 | 31900 | 16200 | 26,7 | 3200 | 1915 |
| L 20 — 24 | | 178,5 | 35800 | 17900 | 26,5 | 3500 | 1915/16 |
| L 30 — 41, 45, 47, 50 | | 198 | 55200 | 35500 | 28,7 | 4000 | 1916 |
| L 42 — 43 | | 196,5 | 55500 | 36400 | 27,7 | 5500 | 1917 |
| L 44 u. 46 | | 196,5 | 55800 | 37800 | 28,9 | 5500 | 1917 |
| L 48, 49, 51, 52, 54 | | 196,5 | 55800 | 39000 | 29,9 | 5500 | 1917 |
| L 53, 55, 56, 58, 60 — 65 | | 196,5 | 56000 | 40000 | 30,2 | 6500 | 1917/18 |
| L 57 u. 59 | | 226,5 | 68500 | 52100 | 28,6 | 8200 | 1917 |
| L 70 — 71 | | 211,5 | 62200 | 44500 | 36,4 | 7000 | 1918 |

losses of the Imperial German Navy were 53. The naval airships made a total of 3,055 flights in 19,929 hours covering some 801,700 miles (1,290,175km). The main roles of the Imperial German Navy's airships were reconnaissance (1,148 sorties) and bombing (306 sorties).

War-time losses amounted to 26 airships lost to enemy action, 14 to bad weather and 12 to fire or explosion. Of this overall total, 19 airships crashed and their entire crews were lost, while 24 resulted in the loss of the airship but not the crew. In

six cases the crews were captured, and in another three cases the crews were interned in neutral countries. Personnel losses amounted to 40 officers and 396 other ranks.

By the end of World War I, 17 airships had been declared obsolete and retired, and as a result there were only nine airships left in service at the time of the Armistice that ended World War I on 11 November 1918. Included in the provisions of the Armistice agreement was the stipulation that these remaining airships were to be handed over to the Allies.

The last word in the development of the Zeppelin airship for naval purposes came in the USA, where the Goodyear-Zeppelin Corporation created the USS Akron (seen here) and USS Macon as helium-filled airships.

# CHAPTER FIVE

# Post-War Revival

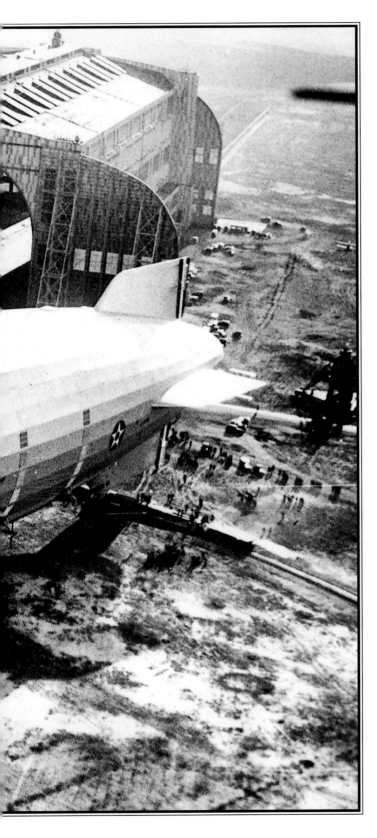

When the armistice of November 1918 brought World War I to an end, the Zeppelin company had under construction at Friedrichshafen the LZ114 airship ordered by the navy for service as the L72. It was hoped that the Allied Armistice Commission would allow the company to retain this airship so that it could resume commercial passenger services.

As a precursor to any such service, the company planned in the greatest secrecy to use this airship for a flight across the Atlantic to New York, in order to reveal the commercial possibilities of the Zeppelin airship. The company therefore informed no foreign government of its plan, but received agreement for the scheme from elements within the German government. As completed, the plan called for the airship to fly down the English Channel by night or, in the event of bad weather, to fly a course round the north of the UK, and thence across the North Atlantic towards the eastern seaboard of the USA. It was only at this stage that permission would be sought by radio for the airship to enter the USA and look for a suitable landing site.

The final details for the flight were being completed in March 1919, and everything was moving smoothly toward a satisfactory conclusion in preparation for a departure in April. As the departure time approached, however, the German government demanded that the flight be cancelled. No reason was given for the ban, but it seems likely that the Allies had learned of the scheme and acted through the German authorities so that the honour of making the first transatlantic flight in an airship would fall to a British machine, the R34, which accomplished the feat some two months later in July 1919.

One of the first actions of the Allies after the end of hostilities was the demand that all modern military equipment should be transferred to their control for examination and subsequent

dispersal as the first step in the satisfaction of the programme of reparations demanded from Germany. The six surviving Zeppelin airships were among the first items seized by the Allied powers: the L61 and LZ120 were transferred to Italy, the L64 and L71 were allocated to the UK, the L113 went to France, and the L30 and L37 were dismantled for delivery to Belgium and Japan respectively. Other airships had been destroyed at their bases by crews emulating the men who, in June 1919, had scuttled their warships while interned in the Orkney Islands.

The Zeppelin company also received orders to hand over the newly completed LZ114. Handed over to France and renamed Dixmude, the new airship was soon launched on a record flight over the Mediterranean, covering some 5,000 miles (8,000km) in a flight time of more than 118 hours. However, during December 1923, the Dixmude crashed into the sea near Sicily while returning from a flight over Africa. The entire crew of 52 were lost.

### UNCERTAIN FUTURE

In overall terms, the German opponents of any resumption of airship activity after World War I pointed to the fact that some 80 airships had been lost during the war by the army and navy, suggesting that there was something inherently unsafe about the concept of the airship. On the other side, the German adherents to the concept of the airship countered with the fact that some 5,000 successful operational sorties had been made by airships during the war, and that some of these sorties had been spectacularly successful. All agreed that the percentage of the men lost

in airship operations had been unfortunately high, but the advocates of the airship's cause countered the arguments of their opponents about the cost of the material losses with the argument that material losses are an inherent part of war, and the loss of an airship should be regarded in the same light as the loss of a warship or a quantity of artillery of approximately the same cost.

At a more practical level, the Zeppelin company felt that the loss of the surviving airships as war reparations was not in fact a bad thing, for these airships had been designed specifically for the military and naval tasks required in the war, and were therefore in no way optimised for adaptation to commercial use. The airships that survived the war were generally of the late-production types schemed to fly at very high altitude and high speed for the bombing and reconnaissance tasks, and would therefore have been both difficult and expensive to convert into cost-effective passenger airships with all the luxury features that would mean the company could demand premium fares.

Keen to re-enter the commercial airship travel business, the Zeppelin company now manufactured two passenger airships with the designations LZ120 and LZ121. These 'Type y' class airships (see Appendix) were considerably smaller than the naval airships they followed on the company's 'production line' at Friedrichshafen and, to provide them with a market, the Zeppelin company reached agreement with a Swedish company, the Svenska Luft Trafik Aktiebolaget, for the inauguration of regularly scheduled airship flights between Berlin and Stockholm. The schedule originally agreed between the two companies envisaged two Zeppelins flying between the German and Swedish capitals on a two-day rotating basis.

The LZ120, named Bodensee, was completed first with a gas capacity of 706,000ft³ (20,000m³), later increased to 796,300ft³ (22,550m³), and with the powerplant of four 245-hp (329-kW) Maybach MB.IVa engines with a maximum speed of 82.5mph (133km/h). It carried a crew of 16 and up to 21 passengers. The Bodensee entered commercial service on 20 August 1919, and within a period of 98 days made 103 flights between Friedrichshafen and Berlin, in the process carrying 2,450 passengers. The one-way flight took six hours, as compared with 18 by train, and the fare was 575 marks.

The extent of the development of the airship during World War I is indicated by the fact that while the Bodensee was no larger in overall terms than the pre-war commercial airships, it carried about twice the payload – 21,164lb (9,600kg), or 42 per cent of its structure weight, at double the speed.

### THE DEBT OF WAR

The LZ121 had just been completed, with the name Nordstern, when the Inter-Allied Air Commission issued instructions that both of the 'Type y' class airships should be handed over to France and Italy as part of Germany's war reparations debt. All airship work at Friedrichshafen again came to a halt, though both the German government and the Zeppelin company hoped that this would be temporary. The LZ120 was delivered to Italy and became the Esperia, but was totally wrecked on its first official appearance. The LZ121, renamed as the Méditerranée, remained in French service up to 1927.

During World War I, non-rigid airships were evaluated and operated by the US Navy in the coastal patrol and related anti-submarine roles, and the importance of these tasks combined with the success of the airships in their fulfilment to persuade the US Navy to invest in larger numbers of non-rigid airships, of which eight classes were eventually employed. In March 1916 Admiral George Dewey and the Department of the Navy recommended the development of rigid airships, and Congress, later authorised the operation and construction of such airships. An early step in this direction was the semi-rigid airship, Roma, which was bought from Italy. This airship had a gas capacity of 1,333,100ft³ (37,750 m³), a length of 410ft (125m) and a maximum diameter of 75ft (23m). It attained a maximum speed of 70mph (113km/h) on the powerplant of six 400-hp (298-kW) engines. After arrival from Italy in a dismantled state, the airship was carefully reassembled in the USA but on a test flight during February 1922 became unmanageable and crashed into high-tension wires near Langley Field, Virginia. Filled with hydrogen, the Roma caught fire and the subsequent explosion caused the deaths of 34 of the 45-man crew.

The British airship R38 was still undergoing tests after the purchase by the US Navy, but was destroyed in 1921 before it had been delivered for service as the ZR-2. Meanwhile, an airship of American design was being built at the Naval Aircraft Factory at Philadelphia, Pennsylvania. This was based on the design of a Zeppelin airship, the L49, which had been created as a high-altitude bomber but then forced down in France during October 1917 and captured intact, thus providing the Allies with the opportunity to examine the very latest in German airship thinking. The ZR-1 (Zeppelin Rigid-1) made its maiden voyage on 4 September 1923 and was named the USS Shenandoah. This airship was 680ft (200m) long, with a maximum diameter of 79ft (24m). It had a maximum gas capacity of 2,115,000ft³ (59,850m³) and was designed with hydrogen as the lifting gas to be used. However, as a result of the many incendiary deaths of hydrogen-filled airships, the USA had decided by this time that only inert helium would be used in its lighter-than-air craft, and the Shenandoah was the first airship in the world to utilise this far safer gas which, being slightly heavier than hydrogen volume for volume, produces about 10 per cent

RIGHT *The USS Shenandoah completed 59 flights before its loss as a result of structural failure in a storm during September 1925. It had proved itself a capable airship, although ultimately too small for the US Navy role planned for it.*

less lift. In other respects the Shenandoah was modelled closely on the L49, from which it differed mainly in the lengthening of the hull by the insertion of a longer central section, the strengthening of the bow so that modern mooring gear could be installed, the redesign of the cruciform arrangement of tail surfaces, the fitting of a top walkway, and the modification of the engine gondolas for the new powerplant of six 300-hp (224-kW) Packard engines, later reduced to five engines in an effort to save weight so that the reduced lift of the helium gas would be offset.

The Shenandoah undertook various naval missions, served as a scouting airship, and made transcontinental demonstration flights, visiting most of the larger cities in the USA. The airship had completed 56 flights, covering some 25,000 miles (40,250km). It had crossed the USA several times and had moored to the masts of the airship tender USS Pakota at the Naval Air Station Lakehurst, New Jersey. It had become a magnificent public relations tool for the US Navy. On its 57th flight, the Shenandoah was scheduled to travel from Lakehurst to St Louis, Minneapolis and Detroit before returning to its base. Caught in a severe storm over Ohio during 3 September 1925, the Shenandoah was tossed about like a scrap of paper.

The control gondola was torn loose from the hull, and the main section of the hull broke into two parts, the forward part then crashing to the ground, the rear section being carried some distance by the storm before it too fell. All the men in this rear section were saved, but of the 43-man crew, the 19 situated in the forward section were killed.

The official report blamed the disaster on the inexperience of the crew, the removal of 7 of the 15 manoeuvring valves and 10 of the 18 automatic gas valves in an effort to avoid wastage of the costly helium gas, and a weakness in the design and/or construction as the airship had apparently encountered unendurable structural stresses in the storm's strong up- and down-draughts.

## A NEW INNOVATION

Rear Admiral William E. Moffett, head of the Naval Airship Service, felt that because the original design, developed in 1915, was for an airship using hydrogen, it was inefficient perhaps 30 per cent beyond the 10 per cent difference in lifting power when adapted for helium. Moffett was still a strong advocate of lighter-than-air craft, especially for a long-range reconnaissance role in conjunction with US naval battle fleets,

LEFT *The USS Shenandoah proved itself a capable and reliable airship and a good public relations tool. The airship crashed in a storm in September 1925.*

ABOVE *Watched by curious children, members of the crew board the USS Akron by means of the airstair door built into the underside of the forward gondola.*

and therefore recommended that, despite the Shenandoah disaster, the US Navy should persevere with the procurement and operation of airships.

This was indirectly the salvation of the Zeppelin company, for the order against which the LZ126 was built was vitally important for the Luftschiffbau Zeppelin, largely as a result of Article 198 of the Treaty of Versailles, signed in 1919 and designed to terminate Germany's involvement in World War I. This article had prohibited further construction of airships in Germany. Zeppelin therefore decided to switch to the manufacture of kitchen utensils, a task in which his experience in the design and manufacture of items from aluminium alloy might allow a profit to be made, but in essence the company's modified function was of no interest at all to the former airship builders. Under the guidance of Eckener, a plan was contrived to persuade the Allies, most particularly the Americans, that they should take an airship instead of the demanded monetary compensation for ships they should have received from the force incarcerated at Scapa Flow but which their crews had scuttled.

Eckener encountered strong resistance from the German government. The fact that the arrangement was to be completed only by the delivery of the airship in the USA persuaded officials that the whole arrangement was fraught with potential dangers,

especially as they were not certain that the airship could be flown safely across the Atlantic and the delivery made. Eventually the Zeppelin team was able to convince the sceptics in the German government, and national authorisation was granted.

The financing of the airship's construction was another difficulty and the government was prepared to offer only one-third of the sum required. Again, the German people responded to a public appeal, as they had several times in Zeppelin's past, and raised the other two-thirds of the finance. A minor problem was that the company's hangar was smaller than the proposed airship, so the airship was reduced from the dimensions originally planned. Other specifications were unaltered.

The resulting LZ126 was of a newly designed streamlined form, and the Dural framework was based on the use of 22 frames for greater stability. The control gondola was built into the lower part of the hull rather than added as a strut-mounted appendage, but the five engine gondolas were suspended on struts. Each of the Maybach engines developed 400hp (298kW), giving the airship a maximum speed of 79mph (127km/h) and a cruising speed of 68mph (109km/h), and a range of 7,765 miles (12,500km).

Eckener believed that a comprehensive series of demonstration flights was necessary to convince people of the safety of airships. The tragic losses of the French Dixmude and British R-38 were still recent memories, and Eckener insisted on proving to them the unqualified safety of Zeppelin travel. So when dismal weather prevailed on the day of the maiden flight, Eckener refused to cancel the trial, thereby showing his complete confidence in the airworthiness of the Zeppelin. This was proved when an accompanying aeroplane was forced to land, leaving the new Zeppelin alone in the air and unscathed by the weather. The airship was hit by lightning, but suffered only a small scorch mark, the electrical charge being carried through the metal skeleton and discharged through the radio antennae.

The delivery flight across the Atlantic Ocean to the USA was, of course, very important and was therefore planned very carefully. The route selected was via the Azores, which was longer than a more northerly route, but offered the probability of better weather. The crew of 28 men was carefully chosen and included no fewer than five experienced airship commanders. Departure was scheduled for early 11 October 1924, but was then delayed by the presence of fog as the damp would have increased the weight of the airship by some 4,400lb (2,000kg) of water attached to the fabric skin, requiring the venting of much lifting gas as ballast water could not be sacrificed to counterbalance the weight of the water on the skin. Thus the departure was rescheduled for the following morning. Heavy cloud hung low over the area and the temperature was 50°F (10°C) as the LZ126 lifted off and, at an altitude of 2,300ft (700m), cleared the cloud cover. The planned route took the airship up the valley of the Rhine to Basle, round the French fortress areas of Belfort and

Besançon, and then across France to the Bay of Biscay. Here the weather was poor, and the airship changed course slightly to fly along the north coast of Spain to Cape St Vincent.

On the second day of the flight, the Zeppelin airship climbed to an altitude of 4,925ft (1,500m), and at noon reached the Azores, where two small sacks of mail were dropped at Terceira. The cloud-concealed mountain of Pico Alto, extending to 13,500ft (4,100m), had to be avoided. Soon the cruisers *USS Detroit* and *USS Milwaukee*, escorts provided by the US Navy, were contacted for weather reports, and Eckener changed course to avoid a region of low pressure and climbed above the probable storm. On the night of 15 October, the crew sighted Sable Island, off Nova Scotia, and knew they had reached North America after an Atlantic crossing of 70 hours.

The airship flew over Boston and New York, circling the Statue of Liberty and returned to fly low over Broadway so that the citizens of New York could see the new airship before it headed for Lakehurst, after a flight of 5,066 miles (8,153km) covered in a time of 81 hours 17 minutes at an average speed of 62mph (100km/h). Nine members of the German crew remained at Lakehurst to assist the Americans in operating what now became the ZR-3, or USS Los Angeles.

An interesting sidelight to the LZ126 programme was the fact that in 1923 it also led to a partnership between Zeppelin and the Goodyear Tire & Rubber Company of Akron, Ohio, when these German and American companies created the Goodyear-Zeppelin joint venture. The Germans were more or less obliged to accept this arrangement because of the aircraft

LEFT *Crew members work on one of the eight 560-hp (418-kW) Maybach engines used to propel the ZRS-4, otherwise known as the USS Akron.*

RIGHT *A tripodal mobile mooring mast was used to capture the US Navy's airships, in this instance the ZRS-5 or USS Macon, before towing them into their hangars in a process that was reversed before the airships could be launched.*

building restrictions imposed upon Germany by the Versailles treaty. Besides the transfer of the patent rights, the deal also involved the employment by the American company of Dr Karl Arnstein, Zeppelin's chief engineer, as well as 12 technical experts.

The first action of the airship's new American crew was to drain the hydrogen from the gas cells in anticipation of the arrival of the Shenandoah, as this airship contained practically the total supply of helium available at that time. The costly gas was then transferred to the 14 gas cells in the Los Angeles, and as a consequence the Shenandoah was rendered inoperable for

the next eight months as the Los Angeles completed a number of flights, two of them extending as far as Bermuda.

The loss of the Shenandoah, and with it the USA's supply of helium, in September 1925 was a great blow to the American public, which nonetheless wanted the US Navy to persevere with the development and operation of large rigid airships. As a result, considerable financial expenditure allowed the production of a new supply of helium, and after it had been filled with the new supply of gas the airship took to the air once more under the command of Captain Charles E. Rosendahl, a survivor of the Shenandoah disaster. During the following three years, the success of the Los Angeles under Rosendahl did much to restore overall confidence in rigid airships.

## NEW CAPABILITIES

The Los Angeles showed in 1926 that it could moor to the depot ship *USS Patoka*, which had been fitted with a special mooring mast. A further step was taken in 1928 when the Los Angeles eased down onto the flight deck of the aircraft carrier *USS Saratoga*, and on 3 July 1929 the Los Angeles itself became an aircraft carrier of altogether different type: as the airship cruised at 78mph (125km/h), Lieutenant A. W. 'Jake' Gordon carefully flew his Vought UO-1 observation biplane along the underside of the airship's hull and engaged a hook (attached to the upper wing of his aeroplane) onto a trapeze fixed to the hull of the airship. This concept aimed to extend the capabilities of the airship by increasing its operational reach with a reconnaissance aeroplane or adding an ability to protect itself with an embarked fighter. It was not a new concept, as the idea had been tested in Germany and the UK during World War I, and the US Army had also conducted some similarly successful trials in 1924, when one of its aircraft hooked onto a non-rigid 'blimp' airship.

Command of the Los Angeles later passed to Captain Herbert V. Wiley and then, in 1930, to Captain Alger H. Dresel, under whom further trapeze trials were undertaken with heavier-than-air craft as different as the Consolidated N2Y-1 trainer and Curtiss XF9C-1 Sparrowhawk fighter.

For many years the Los Angeles flew a great number of people to important events in many parts of the USA, and at the same time the airship provided new crews with a means of perfecting their training in the handling of rigid airships. On only one occasion did the Los Angeles serve as a military machine, the former Allies granting their special permission on this occasion, and this was in the US Navy manoeuvres of 1931. The Los Angeles operated from the *Patoka* off the west coast of Panama, serving as a scout for the fleet defending the Panama Canal.

In June 1932, the Los Angeles was one of the many victims of the 'Great Depression' affecting the USA. It was in this month that the airship was finally decommissioned, and although this was seen at the time as a temporary measure, the airship was only recommissioned for a short time following the loss of the ZRS-4 (otherwise USS Akron) in 1934, before finally being scrapped early in 1940 after acquiring 4,398 flight hours in 331 flights, as well as a further 2,000 hours moored to a mast.

The link between Zeppelin and Goodyear paved the way for the construction in the USA of two other Zeppelin-type rigid airships with the prodigious gas capacity of 6,500,000ft³ (184,000m³). During 1926, the US Navy received Congressional authorisation to proceed with the procurement of two rigid airships intended specifically for the long-range naval reconnaissance role. In order to accommodate these impressive new vessels the ZRS prefix was created, with Z being the US Navy prefix letter for lighter-than-air (in fact Zeppelin), R for rigid and S for scouting. Whereas the service's only

LEFT *The Curtiss F9C Sparrowhawk, launched and recovered by a retractable trapeze associated with an internal hangar, was used to extend the scouting range of the USS Akron and USS Macon.*

RIGHT *Lying flat in its construction position, the large ring frame in the foreground would have been hauled upright before being attached to the growing frame of the USS Macon.*

previous rigid airship of US design and manufacture, the ZR-1, had been a wholly US Navy endeavour designed by the Bureau of Aeronautics and manufactured by the Naval Aircraft Factory, the US Navy decided now to try private enterprise.

The US Navy drafted the specification in terms of performance, strength, safety factors etc. and invited tenders for the detail design and manufacturing process. Such was the importance attached to the programme, that the service received 37 different bids, three of them from Goodyear-Zeppelin (the company created after the American companies joined forces with the German organisation for the use of the latter's patents). Given Goodyear's great experience in the building of airships it was hardly surprising that Goodyear-Zeppelin became the successful bidder. The corporation was therefore awarded a contract in 1928 to built the two 'ZRS-4' class airships, which became the ZRS-4 and ZRS-5, later to receive the names USS Akron and USS Macon respectively.

At first the work on Akron was concentrated on the erection of a vast shed in which the airships would be built, and it was only in November 1929 that work on the assembly of the ZRS-4's structure began as Admiral Moffett drove a gold rivet into the main bulkhead of the airship. Arnstein, the chief designer and formerly the technical director of Zeppelin in Germany, and his staff now faced considerable difficulties, not least because the construction of the

airships was undertaken in the full glare of the American public, which lapped up rumours of sabotage to vital structural components, use of inferior materials, and excessive structural weight. Both the US Navy and the manufacturer rebutted these rumours, which nonetheless persisted until the ZRS-4 proved itself an excellent airship, in every respect better than the German-built ZR-1.

### NEW FEATURES

Important new features included the incorporation of the eight engines inside the hull, with only the propellers projecting, for easier in-flight maintenance and reduced drag. As far as the propellers themselves were concerned, these were not only reversible to provide braking effect during landing if required, but could also be swivelled into the horizontal position to create either upward or downward thrust, which was of great use in the lift-off and landing regimes. Novel was the arrangement of a ladder of condensers on the sides of the hull above each engine for the recovery of water vapour in the engine exhausts: condensed from steam, this water was piped into the airship's ballast tanks to replace the ballast discharged in the course of normal operations, and this helped to mitigate the need to valve-off precious helium gas as the ballast was used.

Whereas previous Zeppelin-designed airships had possessed only one passageway, the ZRS-4 possessed no fewer than three

ABOVE *The LZ127 Graf Zeppelin comes in to land at a German airship base after a test flight.*

LEFT *Flying near Lakehurst, New Jersey, Lieutenant A.W. 'Jake' Gordon approaches the trapeze of the USS Los Angeles on 3 July 1929 for a practice hook-on in his Vought UO-1 biplane, the type that was replaced on the USS Akron and USS Macon by the Curtiss F9C Sparrowhawk.*

internal passageways: two of these were located in the lower part of the hull, which was cross-connected by lateral tunnels, while the third passageway extended along the upper part of the hull. Finally, the ZRS-4 was a real aircraft carrier.

After trials with the ZR-3 had proved the feasibility of the system whereby an aeroplane could hook onto the airship in flight and later fly free of the hook, the ZRS-4 could use a retractable trapeze in flight to catch a sequence of up to five reconnaissance or fighter aircraft for accommodation in a special hangar, measuring 75ft (23m) by 60ft (18m), located inside its huge belly. This capability was considered especially impor-

tant in airships of the 'ZRS-4' class, which were intended to serve as the long-range eyes of the US Navy's primary fleets, with a greater optical horizon provided by their embarked reconnaissance aircraft.

The ZRS-4 was named the USS Akron on 8 August 1931, but the airship then had to undergo a rigorous programme of tests before a first flight could be essayed. Thus, it was only on 13 September 1931 that the ZRS-4's first commander, Captain Rosendahl, could lift off for the airship's first flight. An intensive flight trials effort followed, until on 17 October 1931 the airship was officially taken on US Navy charge.

## A RISKY BUSINESS

Despite a number of minor mishaps, the US Navy felt that the ZRS-4 was an important asset to its surface warfare forces, but the airship was not fated to have a happy career. A typical instance, for which the airship was not directly responsible except in the somewhat superstitious minds of sailors, took place when a landing was not completed: although the men of the ground crew were ordered to release the holding ropes, three sailors held on to them and were carried aloft by the rising airship, two of the men then plunging to their deaths and the third being hauled to safety on board the airship only one hour later.

Once the ZRS-4 had settled into the routine of naval service, the 'trapeze artist' pilots of the airship's complement of Curtiss F9C Sparrowhawk aircraft started to practise the system of hook-ons and releases that allowed them to reach and then depart from the airship. The airship was now under the command of Captain Frank McCord, an officer of proven capability but inexperienced in the handling of large airships.

On 3 April 1933 the ZRS-4 was prepared for a sortie in which it would take bearings on, and check, a number of radio stations along the northern end of the USA's eastern seaboard. On this occasion its F9C-2 aircraft were not embarked, but the airship had one very important passenger in the form of Admiral Moffett. The ZRS-4 lifted off from NAS Lakehurst, New Jersey, in deteriorating weather: conditions were foggy, and thunderstorms were moving into the area. At midnight, the ZRS-4 was far out over the Atlantic Ocean as McCord manoeuvred in a vain effort to keep clear of the worst of the weather. The captain decided to head towards the coast once more. Shortly after this the ZRS-4 was pulled down by a violent down-current of air and struck the surface of the sea with considerable force, cutting all the electrical power in the airship. Some of the crew managed to break out through the airship's canvas skinning to hurl themselves into the icy sea. A German tanker had seen the accident and rescued the three survivors out of the 76-man crew, an officer and two enlisted men.

Less than one month earlier, the ZRS-5 had been completed to a standard that differed from that of the ZRS-4 only in details such as structural revisions that saved 8,000lb (3,600kg) in weight. By October 1933, the ZRS-5 was stationed at the newly established naval air station, named Moffett Field in honour of the admiral who had been lost with the ZRS-4, located at Sunnyvale, California. From this base the new airship and its aircraft were involved in a number of fleet exercises with the Pacific Fleet, and in these exercises the ZRS-5 was highly stressed while making abrupt turns in evasive actions. On 21 April 1934, once more in flight as it headed for a rendezvous with a naval force in the Caribbean Sea, the ZRS-5 was flying through bad weather over the southwestern corner of Texas when a senior engineer realised that one of the large circular inside frames in the stern section, the one that in fact supported the cruciform of fixed tail surfaces, was about to break. Only temporary repairs, using wooden planks, could be implemented in the air, but the airship returned safely to its temporary base at Opalocka, Florida. The ZRS-5 was urgently required for fleet manoeuvres, however, and only a short-term repair was effected.

When the ZRS-5 returned to California after these manoeuvres, it still had only the temporary repair in its tail section. The airship's captain up to this time had been Captain Alger H. Dresel, who was now succeeded by Captain Wiley, a highly experienced airship officer who had previously served in the ZR-1 and ZR-3 as well as the ZRS-4 from which he had been the only surviving officer. The US Navy thought that Wiley was the ideal man to expand the capabilities that the ZRS-5 had already revealed, especially as he was a major enthusiast for the airship/aeroplane combination. Wiley also reintroduced the practice developed in World War I of lowering an observer in a small car through the cover of clouds below the airship.

In November 1934 the ZRS-5 was involved in Pacific naval exercises, and the airship's success seemed to persuade all levels of the US establishment that the operation of rigid airships was now a matter of only very limited danger. On 11 February 1935, the ZRS-5 was aloft once more on routine operations off the coast of southern California. No one on board the airship was worried by the possibility of deteriorating weather as the airship seemed to have proved its ability to survive adverse conditions. On that day and the next the ZRS-5's F9C-2 aircraft were involved in efforts to locate the ships of the 'hostile' fleet, and by mid-morning on 12 February the ZRS-5 had fulfilled its tasks and departed on the return trip to Sunnyvale. Off Cape San Martin the fog grew denser and when, late in the afternoon, the airship was off the lighthouse at Point Star, Wiley decided to head away from the coast and for a period the airship remained out over the sea. It then passed through a storm of rain, and after a crash had been heard the airship began to vibrate, and the helmsman reported that the wheel felt quite slack in his hands. Nobody yet knew that the upper fin, together with the rudder attached to its trailing edge, had become completely detached, but it soon became clear that the situation was becoming desperate as the whole of the tail section began to break up, and the long-neglected damage took its toll on the airship. Soon the ZRS-5 had fallen onto the sea. Two men drowned, but the other 81 crew members climbed onto the floating nose section of the airship, from which they were rescued.

The reaction to this disaster was one of devastation. All American airship construction and operation was immediately cancelled. The ZRS-4 and ZRS-5 had logged 73 and 54 flights respectively, with total flying times of 1,695 and 1,798 hours.

*Ground personnel work overnight to prepare the LZ127
Graf Zeppelin in its hangar for a long-distance flight.*

# CHAPTER SIX

# Boom and Disaster

In the late 1920s and through most of the 1930s, there was considerable argument among those interested in aviation matters about the relative merits of the lighter-than-air airship and the heavier-than-air aeroplane for the civil transport role. The believers in the merits of the airship were sure that the type of craft they favoured was the way to the future for longer-range transport, leaving the shorter-range field to the aeroplane, which had a decided advantage over distances under 600 miles (1,000km).

Among the positive features that the adherents of the airship adduced to their side of the argument were the ability of the airship to float over a given spot (typically near the mooring tower) at very low or even zero speed, to operate with greater safety under adverse weather conditions (such as fog, rain or snow), to operate at night with considerably less perceived noise, and to provide considerably more comfortable and roomy accommodation in a vehicle that thus seemed to combine the most attractive attributes of the ocean liner (comfortable staterooms and impressive public rooms) and the heavier-than-air transport aeroplane (speed between departure and arrival points). There could be no denial of the fact that aircraft in general, and the flying boat in particular, had made considerable strides in the level of their performance and comfort during the 1920s, and a considerable increase in range with the maximum payload was presaged by the payload/range performance of flying boats such as the Dornier Do X.

Dr Hugo Eckener, Chairman of Luftschiffbau Zeppelin, was sure that the long transoceanic crossing was the area of air transport in which the airship could and should excel. Soon after the company had delivered the LZ126 to the USA for naval service as the ZR-3 (USS Los Angeles), Eckener revealed the details of a study that had been undertaken into the potential of the airship as a primary means of transport between Europe and the Americas. He also revealed that the three attributes he believed essential for the long-term feasibility of airship travel were speed (to keep the journey time within reasonable limits), a high level of operational safety, and the combination of low cost (both purchase and operating) and reliability that would make it possible to charge passengers a reasonable fare.

### A TRANSATLANTIC PASSENGER SERVICE

In the transoceanic role, a major saving in time over the present generation of ocean liners was clearly not just possible but already present, as no current liner could cruise at a speed in excess of 30kt (34mph/55km/h) while current airships were capable of cruising at nearly double that speed. Within the same basic field, Eckener was of the opinion that successful airship navigation was more a matter of meteorological appreciation than basic airmanship to plot and steer the best possible course, resulting in transatlantic journey times approximately half of that taken by an ocean liner for the westward crossing, and of about one-third of the liner's time for the eastward crossing, which benefited from the prevailing westerly winds.

Eckener believed that, in its basic aerodynamic, structural and mechanical form, the airship had an essentially good safety record, and that the safety aspect could be enhanced considerably if plentiful supplies of helium gas were made available. This would allow the airship to be filled partially with this inert gas and only partially with hydrogen, which could be contained in an arrangement that would still further reduce the chance of the gas blending with air to create a flammable mixture. Within this context, Eckener believed that petrol engines should be replaced in airship service by diesel engines, and thus carry as their fuel relatively hard-to-ignite heavy oil rather than the readily-ignitable petrol required by the ordinary aircraft-type engines currently used in airships. This too would be a major factor in improving the safety of the airship.

Rather less compelling was Eckener's assertion that there was only a modest degree of danger in trying to moor an airship under adverse weather conditions, while even ocean liners were handicapped in storms. This argument totally ignored the fact that most of the world's major ports are located in natural harbours providing considerable protection from the worst aspects of the weather, whereas the relatively few mooring facilities for airships were located on flat, open ground offering no protection at all from the weather. What could not be denied, however, was that both airships and ocean liners had the endurance to stand off and wait for the moderation of the weather, or to divert over

ABOVE *Ground personnel 'prep' the LZ127 Graf Zeppelin for a flight by filling the airship's gas-fuelled lights.*

RIGHT *Premium rates were paid for the air mail carried by airships such as the LZ127 Graf Zeppelin, which could deliver such mail over longer routes with considerably greater speed than any rival services reliant on trains and ships.*

considerable distances to alternative mooring facilities or ports if necessary, and this was not a capability available to the airliner with its considerably more limited endurance.

Eckener also suggested that when airship travel became the norm for long-distance travel, the mooring facilities for the world's inevitably growing fleet of airships should be built not right outside large urban areas, but slightly further out, at locations offering protection from weather conditions but possessing the potential for the establishment of a railway or other surface link with the nearest metropolitan region. In this regard Eckener drew an analogy with the ocean liner situation, in which these grand vessels did not land their passengers at large cities such as Berlin, Chicago, London and Paris, but rather at the nearest major port enjoying good communications with the target destination.

ABOVE *The Zeppelin company could charge high rates for specialised freight, such as this chimp transported by the LZ127 Graf Zeppelin between Hamburg and New York.*

## COMPETITION THREATENS

Eckener reckoned that the launch of an initial transatlantic service, requiring the construction of three Zeppelin airships as well as the landing facilities and hangars required at each end of the route, would require an outlay of some 35 million marks. He also reckoned that, on the basis of the original schedule of 50 round-trip journeys each year, at 2,500 marks per one-way fare in an airship capable of carrying 30 passengers as well as some 11,000lb (5,000kg), the company's receipts would be 634,000 marks per round trip as compared with outgoings of 400,000 marks per trip. There would also be a more limited income from ancillary aspects of the operation, such as advertising and visits to hangars. In overall terms, Eckener's scheme indicated a return of some 35 per cent on the original capital outlay, which seemed a highly encouraging factor to the banker the company chairman approached for the required capital. It seemed that the only other thing to be sorted out before work started on the grand new project was the reaching of an agreement between the gov-

ernments of Germany and the USA to establish the regulatory framework in which the service would operate.

In the midst of this detailed planning, it came as a considerable shock to all concerned when, on 21 May 1927, Charles A. Lindbergh landed at Paris airport after taking off from Mineola, New York, for a non-stop, solo flight of 3,610 miles (5,810km) across the Atlantic in his Ryan NYP single-engine monoplane. His journey time had been 33 hours 30 minutes. This event captured the imagination of the world in a truly astounding fashion, and although it was realised that this flight was a record-breaking event with little in the way of immediate social or commercial effects, it was also appreciated that where this pioneer had led, soon great numbers of larger, commercial aircraft would almost certainly soon follow. The fact that this was likely to be the case was suggested strongly less than one month later, on 6 June 1927, when Clarence Chamberlain carried the first passenger, Charles Levine, from Mineola over an even longer non-stop distance to the German city of Eisleben in a Bellanca single-engine monoplane. These pioneers were soon succeeded by others who flew across the North Atlantic from the USA and then, over 12–13 April 1928, crossed the North Atlantic in the opposite direction for the first time. This latter feat was accomplished by a Junkers single-engine monoplane in the hands of a crew captained by the Graf Günther von Hünefeld, which took off from Dublin in Ireland and landed at Greenly Island off the coast of Labrador.

Among the public it was perceived that, while these pioneers might be able to cross the North Atlantic, and while this spate of record-breaking might open the possibility to commercial transport services in heavier-than-air craft across this genuinely formidable water barrier, in the short and even medium term the future of long-distance air travel, especially over barriers such as the North Atlantic, lay with the lighter-than-air craft for the reasons rightly promoted by Eckener.

## THE FIRST PLANS

The next step in the development of the Zeppelin concept was therefore the design and manufacture of the first airship intended specifically for the safe transport of a commercially viable payload over a very long distance. The result was the LZ127, which was planned as a long-distance airship, able to carry a large quantity of mail or freight as well as 20 passengers accommodated in conditions of considerable comfort. The overall dimensions of the new Zeppelin airship were limited by the size of the hangar that was available at the company's manufacturing facility at Friedrichshafen. This curtailment on the airship inevitably required a measure of compromise, and the effort to balance the requirements of maximum payload (hence a large hull) and maximum speed (hence a streamlined hull with as many engines possible) resulted in the use of a hull of the largest possible size with only moderately good streamlining and therefore only moderately high speed.

The LZ127 was christened the Graf Zeppelin on 8 July 1928 by Zeppelin's daughter, now the Gräfin Helene von Brandenstein-Zeppelin. The count, who had died of pneumonia on 8 March 1917 in Berlin at the age of 78, would have celebrated his 90th birthday on this very date. This was the culmination of a major design and manufacturing effort, and in this time more than 200,000 visitors had toured the Friedrichshafen factory to see the construction of the new airship. The airship was 776ft (232m) long with a diameter of 100ft (302m) and a gas capacity of 2,650,000ft³ (75,000m³). The airship massed 148,000lb (67,130 kg) and had a typical gross lift of 191,800lb (87,000 kg), so the structure weight was slightly more than 77 per cent of the gross weight. After an allowance had been made for vital elements, such as the fuel, ballast water, 36 crew members etc, the Graf Zeppelin could carry a payload of some 33,100lb (15,000kg), which translated as 20 passengers and 26,400lb (11,975kg) of freight and/or mail. The powerplant comprised five 530-hp (395-kW) Maybach VL-2 engines for a maximum speed of 81mph (130km/h), although the cruising speed for the attainment of the maximum range of 6,214 miles (10,000km) was between 59 and 68mph (95 and 110km/h). The engines were installed in five engine gondolas.

The gas cells were fabricated from fine goldbeater's skin, and the outer covering of the hull was of a specially made, strong but light cotton material protected by several coats of varnish mixed with metal powder. The final coat of this paint gave the hull the greatest possible smoothness and the least possible frictional resistance, and also provided the airship with a metallic appearance that shone in sunlight. The airship's framework was fabricated from Dural, an aluminium/copper alloy that is nearly as strong as steel but only one-third of the weight. An indication of the enormous progress that had recently been made in the field of metallurgy is provided by the fact that while the Dural was of the same specific weight as that used in the LZ126, it was one-fifth stronger.

A long corridor ran the entire length of the LZ127's lower hull, and provided simple access to all spaces. There was also another longitudinal walkway, located somewhat higher in the hull, which provided the crew with access to the gas cells for checking and maintenance purposes, and also allowed the reinforcement of the basic structure with cross bracing between the 16 frames that were the heart of the structure.

BELOW *During the late 1920s, the Zeppelin company had facilities for the construction and maintenance of one large and one medium airship at its works at Friedrichshafen on Lake Constance.*

As fuel for the engines, the Graf Zeppelin carried not liquid petrol but a gas mixture (propylene, methane, acethane, acetylene, butylene and hydrogen) known as *Blaugas* ('blue gas'). This allowed the required fuel to be carried in a volume only about two-thirds of that which would have been needed for petrol. The fuel tanks were located below the gas cells for the hydrogen lifting gas and, being only some 9 per cent heavier than air, offered the considerable advantage of not requiring the venting of significant quantities of lifting gas as it was consumed, which would have been necessary in order to prevent the airship from climbing as it lightened, if petrol had been used as the fuel. The same factor was also evident during the airship's landing. As a sop to the fears of the officials of the government, which had contributed 1.1 million marks to the cost of the airship's construction, test flights were made with petrol rather than Blaugas.

### THE GRAF ZEPPELIN'S MAIDEN FLIGHT

The Graf Zeppelin's first test flight was made on 18 September 1928 under the command of Eckener, and lasted for 3 hours 15 minutes. This initial foray into the air was deemed so successful that the first long-range test flight was rescheduled for the next day. The Graf Zeppelin lifted off at 7.30 a.m. and steered a course toward Zürich in Switzerland. The good performance of the airship meant that the small Klemm aeroplane, serving as observer and escort, was soon outdistanced. Soon Basle and Freiburg came into view and were passed as the airship proceeded on a northerly course that now took it over Mannheim, Ludwigshafen, Mainz and Frankfurt. Over Darmstadt, the air-

ship started to climb as the weight of the petrol remaining in the tanks declined, and lifting gas had to be vented in compensation. As the airship reached Stuttgart, the crew paid their respects to the late Ferdinand von Zeppelin by hovering over his tomb and dropping a wreath. The airship then turned south for the return flight to the base at Friedrichshafen.

The third test flight was made to determine the airship's turning radius and its climb performance under all power conditions. Experiments were also made with radio navigation equipment. On the fourth flight several important German scientists as well as foreign dignitaries and airship experts were carried, and trials were also made with Blaugas. For the fifth flight, Eckener flew the airship north over Ulm and then Nuremberg. Here the crew received a radio message about adverse weather over Berlin, so Eckener changed his plan to fly over the German capital and instead directed the Graf Zeppelin over Würzburg, Frankfurt, Köln, and Düsseldorf. During the night the airship flew over Rotterdam in the Netherlands and, after crossing the English Channel and southern part of the North Sea, cruised over Lowestoft and Yarmouth on the east coast of England before

RIGHT *The mooring of the airship bow to a mast was essential so that the airship could ride with the wind and thereby have no undue stresses imposed on its structure.*

BELOW *The controllability of the LZ127 Graf Zeppelin meant that the airship could be posed safely for publicity photographs. Here the airship's bumper trails through the calm waters of Lake Constance.*

turning back to Bremen, Flensburg (Eckener's place of birth) Kiel, Hamburg and then Berlin, whose citizens were finally treated to the magnificent sight of the great airship as it cruised over their city. Eckener released a small parachute-fitted bouquet into the garden of the palace where President Paul von Hindenburg was celebrating his 81st birthday. On its return flight, the airship crossed over the cities of Leipzig, Dresden, Chemnitz and Nuremberg for a second time before landing at Friedrichshafen after a flight of 34 hours 30 minutes and 1,950 miles (3,140km).

### NAVIGATING THE WORLD

The airship was now thought ready for its first transatlantic flight to New York. The company had by this time received a considerable number of reservations, and, from these, 20 passengers were selected for the inaugural service, which also carried 66,000 letters and postcards carrying special commemorative stamps, as well as some high-value freight. Poor weather reports delayed the departure by one day, and thus it was on 11 October 1928 that the Graf Zeppelin departed at 7.55 a.m. for the first commercial passenger air service across the North Atlantic. The airship's route passed over Basle, down the valley of the River Rhône, across the western Mediterranean, past Gibraltar, over the islands of the Madeira and Azores groups, and then across the Atlantic to reach Bermuda and finally the eastern seaboard of the USA. After making landfall, the Graf Zeppelin overflew Washington DC, where the first lady, Mrs Grace Coolidge, had invited friends to see the event from the White House. It then passed over Baltimore, Philadelphia and New York before arriving at Lakehurst at 5.38 p.m. on 15 October. The airship had been aloft for 111 hours 44 minutes.

On the journey home, the Graf Zeppelin flew a more northerly and shorter route across the North Atlantic. It lifted off on 29 October with 24 passengers, and ran into very thick fog over Newfoundland and then ran into as violent a storm as any of the crew could remember. The airship rode out the weather without problem, and reached Friedrichshafen after 71 hours 51 minutes in the air and a distance of some 4,560 miles (7,340km).

During the winter of 1928–29, the Graf Zeppelin was thoroughly overhauled and revised in a number of limited respects. There followed a number of short flights before, on 24 March 1929, the airship departed on a trip to the Middle East with 28 passengers. The journey took them over Marseilles, Corsica, Rome, Crete, Haifa, Jerusalem, Athens and Vienna before returning to Friedrichshafen after 81 hours 30 minutes in the air and coverage of some 4,970 miles (8,000km). One month later,

RIGHT *This magnificent view of Manhattan, taken from the observation lounge on board the LZ127 Graf Zeppelin, highlights the draw for many passengers of airship travel.*

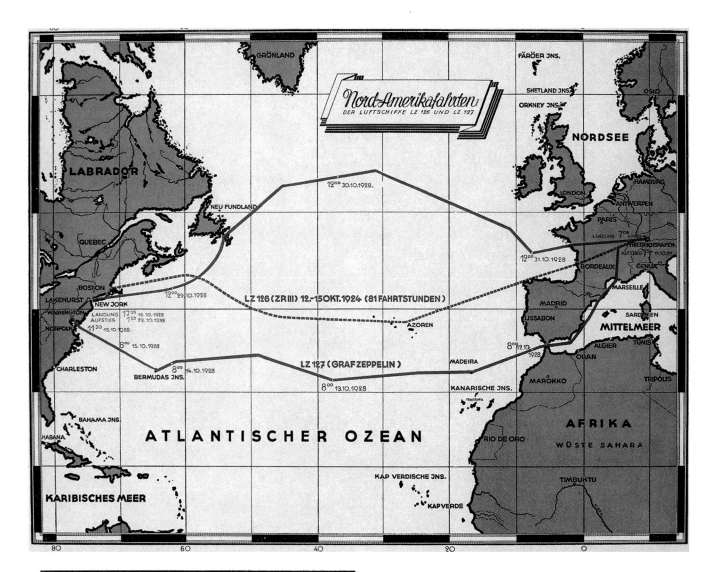

ABOVE *Atlantic crossings were undertaken by the LZ126 and the LZ127 Graf Zeppelin in 1924 and 1928 respectively.*

LEFT *In April 1931 the LZ127 Graf Zeppelin undertook a round-trip from southern Germany to Egypt, passing along the western side of Italy on the outward leg and returning by the eastern side of the country.*

coast of France, and after emergency repairs the airship returned to its base in the southern Germany for repairs.

On 1 August 1929, the Graf Zeppelin flew across the Atlantic to Lakehurst to collect several passengers for a 'round-the-world cruise' that had long been planned. This epoch-making service departed from Friedrichshafen during 15 August 1929 with 18 passengers and two newspaper reporters as the human cargo, and 1,100lb (500kg) of mail and freight as the rest of the cargo. The cruise initially took them by way of Leipzig, Berlin, Stettin, Danzig, and Königsberg to the border of the USSR, over which the airship flew in an almost straight line and at a high speed thanks to the provident arrival of a strong tailwind. Reaching the Far East, the airship had to navigate round a typhoon as it

a similar but shorter flight was made, and then a third Middle Eastern flight included a landing at Cairo in Egypt. Other journeys, undertaken in response to passenger demand, included round-trips to Italy and Spain. A second flight to the USA failed, as a result of mechanical problems, at Toulon on the southern

approached Japan, although the continued presence of strong tailwinds meant that the speed over the ground was still high. After a distance of 7,000 miles (11,300km), covered in a time of 101 hours, the airship reached Tokyo on 19 August and landed at a nearby naval base. The flight lifted off once more on 23 August and headed out across the Pacific, which was largely obscured by fog and cloud for the two days of the crossing, before passengers and crew alike were delighted to see landfall marked by a superb view of the Golden Gate bridge at San Francisco, California. The airship now headed south to Los Angeles, where it arrived in a time of 79 hours from lift-off at Tokyo. The Graf Zeppelin remained for only one day at Los Angeles, lifting off at midnight for the passage across the USA via Chicago, Cleveland and Detroit to Lakehurst, the 2,995 miles (4,820km) of this leg of the journey being accomplished in 52 hours. At this stage Eckener, with business matters requiring his attention in the USA, relinquished command of the Graf Zeppelin to Ernst Lehmann, who guided the airship across the Atlantic to a landing at its Friedrichshafen base on 4 September 1929.

In six stages, the Graf Zeppelin had flown some 21,250 miles (34,200km), and had completed its round-the-world flight without any major technical problem or delay.

ABOVE *In its classic 'round-the-world' flight of 1929, the LZ127 Graf Zeppelin made several landings, including one at Tokyo, where the airship caused an enormous stir.*

BELOW *Another of the journeys completed by the LZ127 Graf Zeppelin, in this instance during 1929, was the circumnavigation of the Iberian peninsula.*

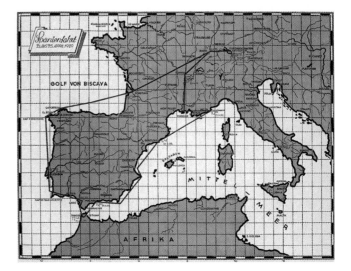

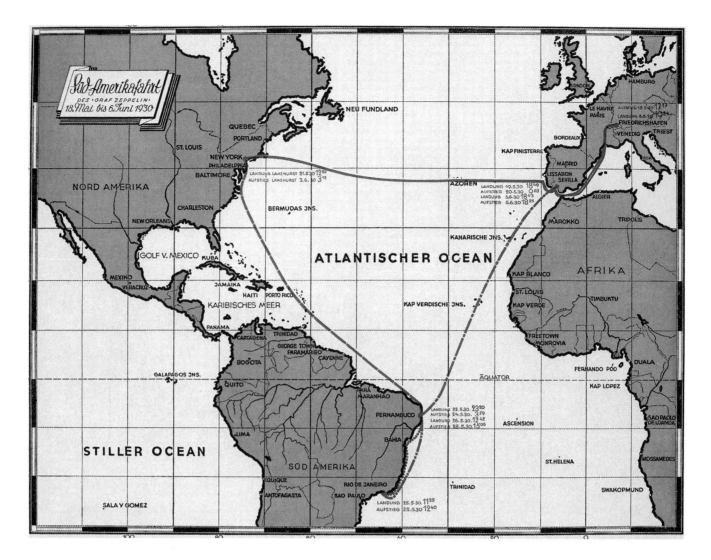

Süd-Amerikafahrt
DES ‹GRAF ZEPPELIN›
18. Mai bis 6. Juni 1930

After another refit during the winter, the Graf Zeppelin left Friedrichshafen on 18 May 1930 with a payload of 22 passengers. This was to be yet another ambitious voyage, and the airship's first port of call was Seville in southern Spain, where a landing was made during the evening after the airship had been forced to detour over Morocco and Tangiers to await the cool of the day's end, after reaching its destination at an average speed of 125mph (200km/h) with the aid of a potent tailwind. From Seville, the airship cruised for 62 hours across the central part of the Atlantic before it landed at Recife de Pernambuco in Brazil, from which it lifted off once more at midnight for the journey south to Rio de Janeiro, where the wildly enthusiastic crowds were prevented only with the greatest difficulty from celebrating with their normal and, in the circumstances, highly dangerous bombardment of fireworks! The Graf Zeppelin then returned to Pernambuco. From here the cruise's course took the airship north via Natal toward Cuba, where a landing was scheduled but cancelled as a result of adverse weather, and so on to Lakehurst for a landing on 31 May.

The Graf Zeppelin left Lakehurst on 3 June and flew low over New York before heading out over the North Atlantic to Seville,

ABOVE *One journey, undertaken by the LZ127 Graf Zeppelin in 1930, passed along the southeastern coast of Spain before crossing the Atlantic to a landfall in Brazil, and then north to the USA for a return trip across the Atlantic.*

RIGHT *A German map of the 'round-the-world' flight of the LZ127 Graf Zeppelin, which was completed with no technical problems.*

where it arrived after 61 hours in the air. From Seville the airship's course home took it up the Rhône valley, where heavy weather meant a measure of discomfort for the passengers and crew but no problem for the airship. It went on to Friedrichshafen for an arrival on 6 June after the completion of a triangular journey of considerable length. By the time the Graf Zeppelin was laid up for its winter refit, it had completed 130 flights.

### THE NORTH POLE

On 24 July 1931, and with Eckener once more in command, the Graf Zeppelin lifted off for an exploration flight over the North Pole, planned as the logical successor to the 1910 expe-

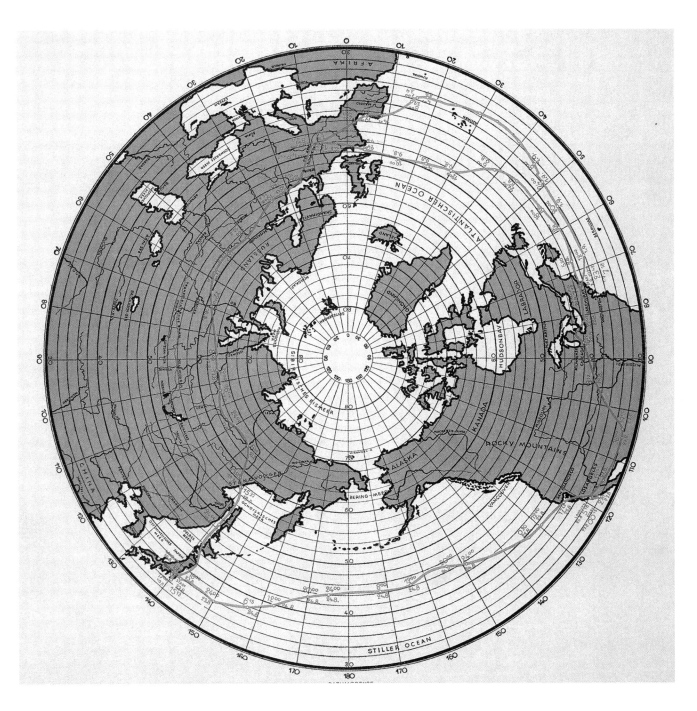

dition undertaken by von Zeppelin. Among the eminent scientists and explorers on board the airship were Professor Samoilovitz, the leading Soviet expert on the Arctic, the celebrated explorer Lincoln Ellsworth, and a number of physicists, biologists and surveyors wanting to examine surface conditions in the Arctic, and to measure all manner of data such as the magnetic field, temperature, air pressure and humidity.

At Leningrad the airship was prepared for its expedition. Nearly all of the standard passenger accommodation was stripped out of the Graf Zeppelin, and the space thus provided and the weight thereby saved allowed the carriage of a mass of scientific instrumentation. Leaving Leningrad and approaching the Arctic Ocean via Arkhangel'sk, the airship headed north and

off Franz Josef Land linked up with the icebreaker *Malygin*, which had another famous Arctic explorer, Umberto Nobile, on board. The airship and the Soviet icebreaker joined forces on 27 July in a bay at Hooker Island, where the airship descended to float on its bumper bags. North of Franz Josef Land the exploration team met nothing but solid pack ice. They discovered that the Gamsworth and Albert Edward islands, shown on most maps of the time, were just names without any real existence, and that on Nikolai II Island there were large glaciated mountains. Fog and thick cloud now intervened, and the airship turned east toward Severnaya Zemlya and then south toward the Taymyr peninsula. The airship next turned west across the Kara Sea and the large island of Novaya Zemlya, finally retracing its outward course to pass close to Arkhangel'sk and Leningrad before reaching Berlin after a time of 145 hours 30 minutes and a distance of 8,300 miles (13,350km) in the air.

Although the need to generate revenue by meeting customer demand had meant that the airship was used for a number of special events, such as the journeys to the Middle East and the Arctic, which had also been considerable publicity coups, Eckener was still firmly convinced that the airship's real métier was the operation of long-distance scheduled services between Germany and the Americas. There followed three flights to South America in 1931 and another nine in 1932. This preponderance of services to South America recognised the fact that, while North Atlantic services could be delayed and buffeted by adverse weather at virtually any time of the year, South Atlantic services generally enjoyed the benefit of more benign weather and the advantageous effects of the trade winds to shorten journey times and thus economise on fuel: clear advantages to the operation's 'bottom line'.

### DESIGN FOR COMFORT

One of the keys to the success of the Graf Zeppelin's commercial operations was the very high degree of comfort that the passengers could expect. There was no crowding, and the passenger

accommodation comprised the rear section of the control gondola, which was lengthened into the underside of the airship's hull to provide both luxurious private staterooms and elegant public rooms. The public rooms were fitted with large windows angled in at their bottoms so that the passengers could watch the world below from their easy chairs, which were fully upholstered. The dining room was every bit as handsome as that of any ocean liner, with monogrammed crockery and cutlery, attentive service, a good wine list and cooking by first-class chefs using only the best ingredients.

The Graf Zeppelin completed 25 commercial flights from Friedrichshafen to Rio de Janeiro, and of these some 20 lasted between 90 and 99 hours. Some 23 flights in the opposite direction were completed, 15 lasted between 100 and 110 hours, with six completed in a shorter time and only two in a longer time. On the North Atlantic route between Friedrichshafen and North America, the westward leg was generally slowed by the prevailing westerly winds while the eastward leg benefited from these winds for a faster passage: the flights from Lakehurst aver-

BELOW *After its magnificent 'round-the-world' flight, the LZ127 Graf Zeppelin was welcomed back to base at Friedrichshafen in southern Germany.*

aged 70 hours, while that from Akron took 102 hours for an eastward average of just over 76 hours; in comparison the westward average was 96 hours.

An early conclusion drawn from the services to North America was that the Graf Zeppelin was not capable of operating with the reliability needed for any real type of scheduled service, and would therefore have to be replaced by a larger, faster and generally more reliable airship if the scheduled service was to become possible and, more importantly, profitable.

Between 18 September 1928 and 10 December 1935, the Graf Zeppelin made 505 flights and covered more than 1 million miles (1.6 million km). Nearly all of these flights had been incident-free, the major exception being the occasion in 1935 when, on an out-and-back journey from Friedrichshafen, the airship had been unable to land at Pernambuco as a result of the revolution taking place there at the time. Lehmann decided to remain in the air until the situation had stabilised, and in fact loitered in the vicinity until a landing was achieved after the airship had been in the air for 118 hours 40 minutes. During this time the airship had been circling off the Brazilian coast, the crew had lifted essential supplies from the steamship *Espana*.

By the time the Graf Zeppelin had completed this journey, it was becoming clearer, if not actually clear, that the days of the airship as the primary means of transoceanic air travel were approaching their end. By this time large four-engined flying boats from the Sikorsky and Martin stables in the USA had

ABOVE *The LZ127 Graf Zeppelin tied to the mobile mooring mast in the US Navy airship hangar at Lakehurst, New Jersey.*

achieved their first payload-carrying flights across the Pacific and Atlantic Oceans.

Even so, Eckener felt that there was still scope for successful services by airships offering greater payload and performance than the Graf Zeppelin. The airship planned for this task was therefore a major improvement over the Graf Zeppelin, and with two such airships Eckener reckoned that a commercially viable weekly schedule between Germany and the USA could be established.

### THE HINDENBURG

The LZ129 was 804ft (240m) long with a diameter of 135ft (41m) and a gas capacity of 7,063,000ft³ (199,900 m³). The airship massed 287,000lb (130,000kg) and had a typical gross lift of 511,500lb (230,000 kg), so the structure weight was slightly more than 56 per cent of the gross lift. After allowance had been made for vital elements such as the fuel, ballast water, 40 crew members etc, the LZ129 could carry a payload of some 41,900lb (19,000 kg), which translated as 50 passengers weighing 15,000lb (6,750kg) and 26,000lb (11,700 kg) of freight and/or mail. The powerplant comprised four 1,050-hp (783-kW) Maybach L-O-F6 (later renamed as Daimler-Benz DB 602) engines for a maximum

speed of 84mph (135km/h), and the maximum range was some 10,250 miles (16,500km).

The four engines, each installed in its own gondola, were of the diesel type running on heavy oil, and this was a significant factor in reducing the fire hazard. For the same reason consideration was given to the use of helium as the lifting gas carried in the outer cells, although most of the 16 gas cells were still to be filled with the cheaper hydrogen gas, which also could lift 16.5 tons more than helium. In fact helium never became available as the Americans reserved all their production for use in their own airships.

The airship could carry a maximum of 70 passengers, although the normal maximum load was only 50 passengers, who could thereby be provided with a greater level of comfort, or even luxury. Most of the passenger cabins, each of them equipped with a shower, were located inside the airship and were decidedly larger than those of the Graf Zeppelin. There were 20 deluxe staterooms on the outside of the B deck in the centre of the airship, which was linked with the A deck above it by two stairways. On the A deck was a spacious dining room that measured some 33ft (10m) by 16ft (5m) with seating for 34 passengers, a bar and smoking room, and a writing and reading room. The public rooms even accommodated a specially built Blüthner piano weighing only 112lb (50kg). The outsides of the A deck were used for 50-ft (15-m) promenade decks with large windows that sloped inward from top to bottom so that the passengers had the benefit of truly magnificent downward views. The catering for the dining room was the responsibility of a chef and five assistants working in an all-electric kitchen, and there was also stowage for 250 bottles of fine wine.

A factor that elicited considerable and approving comment from the passengers was the general quietness of the airship's public rooms and promenades, which was measured at a level of only 51 dB, 8 dB quieter than the equivalent spaces on an ocean liner, and heavier-than-air craft and trains were considerably more noisy than even the ocean liner. Another factor that excited approval was the airship's relative immunity to the movements of outside air currents and other meteorological conditions. This meant that the airship provided a very smooth ride with an almost total absence of air sickness.

It is interesting to note that in order to maximise the comfort of the passengers and the spaciousness of the rooms available to them, the designers allowed an area of 121ft$^2$ (11m$^2$) for each passenger, whereas the comparable figure for a contemporary airliner provided 18ft$^2$ (2m$^2$); the equivalent volumes were 1,130ft$^3$ (32m$^3$) for the airship and 148ft$^3$ (4.2m$^3$) for the airliner.

The LZ129 made its maiden flight on 4 March 1936 with 87 people on board. The new airship lifted cleanly into the air, and the engines were started only after the airship had reached an altitude of 330ft (100m), being barely audible to the personnel on the command gondola under the forward part of the hull's underside. The airship cruised over the Bodensee and the area immediately round it for some three hours and then returned to its base. A second test flight followed on the next day, when the airship lifted off and in an eight-hour trial cruised

LEFT *An aerial photograph of Friedrichshafen taken from the LZ127 Graf Zeppelin.*

ABOVE *Soviet ground personnel assist in the handling of the airship during the 1930 journey of the LZ127 Graf Zeppelin to Moscow.*

RIGHT *An aerial view of the war memorial in Leipzig from the observation lounge of the LZ127 Graf Zeppelin.*

over Bad Tölz, Munich and Augsburg before returning to Friedrichshafen. A third flight of only short duration completed the airship's test programme, but under the command of Lehmann the airship undertook a fourth proving flight, this lasting for 30 hours and extending over much of southern Germany before Lehmann landed the airship to take on board some 101 officials and passengers on a demonstration flight that ended at the airship's new base, a new hangar built at Löwenthal, only a short distance from Friedrichshafen.

By now named Hindenburg, the new airship and the Graf Zeppelin lifted off on 22 March 1936 to undertake a propaganda campaign designed to suggest that the citizens of Germany should vote for the selection of Adolf Hitler for a second term as chancellor of the country. Remaining in the air for four days, together with the intervening three nights, the Hindenburg dropped a vast number of pro-Hitler leaflets and used specially installed loudspeakers to broadcast martial music and pro-Nazi propaganda.

The Hindenburg landed after it had been in the air for 75 hours, and in that time it had covered 4,100 miles (6,600km), which was slightly less than the Graf Zeppelin.

The Hindenburg was scheduled to enter service in 1936, and in preparation for this fact the Deutsche Zeppelin Reederei, as the revived airship transport company was designated, co-

operated with two other airlines, the Deutsche Lufthansa in Europe and the Condor Syndikat in South America, to create the framework in which the two available Zeppelin airships would be operated for a regular passenger and mail schedule between Germany and South America. The schedule was based on a two-week alternating cycle, with the Hindenburg starting its initial service on 31 March 1936 from southern Germany to the newly established facility at Santa Cruz, some 35 miles (55km) from Rio de Janeiro. This first service left on schedule, and as part of its planned operational method the airship was flown through heavy rain so that water, caught in channels along the sides of the airship's hull, could be collected and ducted into the ballast tanks. Another feature of this first service was the use of the uprated powerplant of 1,320-hp (984-kW) diesel engines, and these engines ran well to ensure that the airship completed its 13,500-mile (21,700-km) round trip on 10 April in a flying time of 216 hours. By the time the Hindenburg had returned, the Graf Zeppelin was already well on its way to South America, in the course of which it completed its 112th flight across one of the world's great oceans.

The Hindenburg's next destination was North America, and it lifted off from the Rhein-Main airfield, which had been selected as the starting point for the service as its altitude of nearly 360ft (110m) allowed the airship to be launched with

ABOVE *The ultimate airship to enter full service was the LZ129 Hindenburg. Everything about this magnificent airship seemed to be 'right' and to herald the birth of airship travel as a fully practical proposition. Its loss came as a severe blow.*

about 13,230lb (6,000kg) more lifting capability than was possible from the Löwenthal base that lay at an altitude of about 985ft (300m). The flight to Lakehurst took only 62 hours 38 minutes, knocking 18 hours 36 minutes off the best time recorded by the Graf Zeppelin, and in the process setting a new airship record for a crossing of the North Atlantic. After a short time in the USA, the airship returned to Germany with a payload of 55 passengers, 155,000 postal items and 2,645lb (1,200kg) of freight. Aided by the prevailing westerly winds, the trip was accomplished in only 49 hours 14 minutes, reducing the Graf Zeppelin's best time by 6 hours 9 minutes.

## THE DREAM BECOMES A REALITY

Over the rest of 1936, the Hindenburg completed eight further round-trip flights to the USA, averaging a time of 63 hours 42 minutes for the westbound leg and 51 hours 46 minutes for the eastbound leg. The best of the eastward trips, between 9 and 11 August, was achieved in a mere 42 hours 53 minutes, and in the course of this flight a speed of 188mph (303km/h) was recorded with a strong tailwind. The airship's record for 1936 revealed a total of 3,530 passengers and 66,100lb (29,750kg) of post and freight.

By this time a practical passenger service between Germany and the Americas had become a reality and, in the eyes of the

Zeppelin company and a large number of other believers in the airship concept, the future of airship transport seemed good, especially as the threat from heavier-than-air craft had yet to materialise in any meaningful way for these long-range flights.

If 1936 had marked the beginning of a promising operational career for the Hindenburg, 1937 looked set to mark the new airship's emergence into a full capability with a year's schedules already well booked. The Hindenburg started the year with a round-trip service to Rio de Janeiro, and was next to undertake the inauguration of the regularly scheduled service between Frankfurt and Lakehurst: 18 such round-trip flights had been planned for the year. The airship departed from Rhein-Main airport on 3 May on its flight to the USA, and although on its previous 10 flights it had carried 1,002 passengers, on this outward leg of the service it was carrying a mere 36 passengers as well as a crew of 61 officers and men. Many of them were on board the airship to train as part of the crew earmarked for the LZ130, the Hindenburg's sister ship, which was currently under construction at Friedrichshafen. The abundance of talent and experience on board the Hindenburg was reflected in the fact that there were four licensed airship captains including the airship's commander, Captain Max Pruss, and Ernst Lehmann.

### THE FINAL CHAPTER

The progress of the Hindenburg toward the USA was delayed by a storm over the English Channel and then another storm over the North Atlantic. On reaching the area of Newfoundland, which lies slightly to the north of the track that had originally be planned, the airship's commander received the radioed information that his airship would probably have to endure still further delay as there was heavy rain and an imminent thunderstorm in the region of Lakehurst. The airship progressed via Boston and the northeast coast of the USA to pass over Manhattan at about 3.00 p.m. with a view to reaching Lakehurst at about 6.00 p.m. The weather was still adverse, however, and the landing was delayed for an hour.

It was 7.25 p.m. when the Hindenburg made its final approach to Lakehurst in conditions typified by a fine drizzle. The landing ropes were dropped from the airship's bow, and one of the US Navy's foremost airship captains, Commander Charles E. Rosendahl, standing at the foot of the tall mooring mast, later recalled that 'everything was proceeding in an entirely

normal manner'. Pruss was clearly in no doubt about the conditions, for his experience in 900 flights had included a large number of more adverse, indeed stormy, weather conditions including a landing in the L11 during a violent thunderstorm during the course of World War I. The forthcoming landing was therefore nothing unusual for Pruss.

Then it all went wrong. Rosendahl saw 'a small burst of flame' on the upper part of the hull just forward of the upper fin's leading edge. This little bloom of flame grew with amazing speed into a large virtually explosive fire like a 'million magnesium flares', as it was described in a radio report on the landing by Herbert Morrison, who continued to report with growing distress as the tragedy unfolded. In only 32 seconds the airship, now little more than a mass of flame licking round exposed structural members, collapsed onto the ground in a heap that continued to burn for some three hours before all the heavy oil fuel had been consumed.

Despite the devastating heat and great speed of the disaster, some 61 men and women escaped from the Hindenburg, but 36 others did not survive, including Lehmann, who died

BELOW *The end of the airship age may be said to have come on 6 May 1937, when the LZ129 Hindenburg caught fire and crashed as it approached the US Naval Air Station at Lakehurst, New Jersey.*

of his injuries in hospital. There followed a protracted and exhaustive inquiry into the cause of the disaster. The two most likely culprits were thought to be a lightning strike or sabotage. The inquiry was unable to state an exact cause, although more modern research has proposed a strong case that the real cause was poor conductivity in the airship's envelope. This comprised large numbers of fabric panels, doped with a material containing zinc and magnesium, laced together to form the taut covering. The theory, which seems to explain all of the events, postulates that the airship's final progress through the dissipating thunderstorm may have led to a build-up of static electricity, some of which was discharged via wet lacing to create areas of different potential that were then equalised by a discharge of static electricity. This then ignited the metallically-doped fabric, leading to the bursting of the gas cells and the subsequent ignition of the escaping hydrogen after it had started to mix with the air. Whatever the cause of the disaster, its very public nature and the totality of the whole event effectively spelled the end for commercial airship operations.

At the time of the Hindenburg's loss, the Graf Zeppelin was near the Canary Islands on its return to Germany. After Captain von Schiller had landed the airship at the end of this journey, the Graf Zeppelin was grounded. It had completed 590 flights in which it had carried 13,110 passengers and flown 1,054,000 miles (1,697,000km). After nine years of successful service, the Graf Zeppelin ended its days as a museum exhibit at Frankfurt. The Hindenburg had flown 63 services, in the course of which it had carried 3,059 passengers and covered 209,500 miles (337,300km). Between them, the Graf Zeppelin and the Hindenburg had completed 173 crossing of the Atlantic Ocean and delivered 103,600lb (47,000kg) of mail and 84,400lb (38,200kg) of freight.

At this disastrous time for the Zeppelin company, the LZ130 was being completed as a sister to the Hindenburg for service from the autumn of 1937. The Graf Zeppelin II, as it was to be named, was then completed relatively slowly and finally made its initial flight on 14 September 1938. The airship completed 30 test flights under the command of Captain Hans von Schiller, but was never used publicly and remained inactive throughout the first part of World War II until, with the Graf Zeppelin, it was scrapped in May 1940 and reduced to scrap for salvage. During World War II the hangars and all airship construction facilities were totally destroyed by bombing, and in 1945 the Allies ordered the liquidation of the Zeppelin company.

RIGHT *Given the extent and speed of the fire that consumed the LZ129 Hindenburg, it is surprising that there were any survivors at all.*

# Appendix: technical details

| Class | Number & designations | First flight | Powerplant | Gas capacity | Length | Maximum diameter | Typical empty weight | Typical gross lift | Typical disposable load | Comp-lement | Speed | Range | Static ceiling |
|---|---|---|---|---|---|---|---|---|---|---|---|---|---|
| a | one airship: LZ1 | 2 July 1900 | 2 x 14-hp (10.4-kw) Daimler N1899 petrol engines | 399,054ft³ (11,300m³) of hydrogen in 17 gas cells | 419ft 11¼in (128m) | 38ft 4⅜in (11.70m) | 22,707lb (10,300kg) | 28,880lb (13,100kg) | 6,173lb (2,800kg) | 5 | 16.99mph (27.34km/h) | 174 miles (280km) | 2,135ft (650m) |
| b | one airship: LZ2 | 17 January 1906 | 2 x 80-hp (59.6-kW) Daimler H4L petrol engines | 367,270ft³ (10,400m³) of hydrogen in 16 gas cells | 419ft 11¼in (128m) | 38ft 4⅜in (11.7m) | 20,392lb (9,250kg) | 26,565lb (12,050kg) | 6,173lb (2,800kg) | 7 | 24.6mph (39.59km/h) | 684 miles (1,100km) | 2,790ft (850m) |
| b | one airship: LZ3 | 9 October 1906 | 2 x 85-hp (63.4-kW) Daimler H4L petrol engines | 399,055ft³ (11,300m³) of hydrogen in 16 gas cells | 419ft 11¼in (128m) | 38ft 4⅜in (11.7m) | 20,392lb (9,250kg) | 28,924lb (13,120kg) | 8,532lb (3,870kg) | 7 | 33.55mph (53.99km/h) | 684 miles (1,100km) | 2,790ft (850m) |
| b | one airship: LZ3A | 23 October 1908 | 2 x 105-hp (78.3-kW) Daimler J4 petrol engines | 430,835ft³ (12,200m³) of hydrogen in 17 gas cells | 446ft 2⅛in (136m) | 38ft 4⅜in (11.7m) | 22,751lb (10,320kg) | 31,195lb (14,150kg) | 8,444lb (3,830kg) | 7 | 33.55mph (53.99km/h) | 684 miles (1,100km) | 2,887ft (880m) |
| c | two airships: LZ4; LZ5 | 20 June 1908 | 2 x 105-hp (78.3-kW) Daimler J4 petrol engines | 529,715ft³ (15,000m³) of hydrogen in 17 gas cells | 446ft 2⅛in (136m) | 42ft 8in (13m) | 28,108lb (12,750kg) | 38,360lb (17,400kg) | 10,251lb (4,650kg) | 11 | 34.67mph (55.79km/h) | 901 miles (1,450km) | not available |
| d | one airship: LZ6 (army ZIII) | 25 August 1909 | 2 x 115-hp (85.7-kW) Daimler J4L petrol engines | 529,715ft³ (15,000m³) of hydrogen in 17 gas cells | 446ft 2⅛in (136m) | 42ft 8in (13m) | 29,872lb (13,550kg) | 38,360lb (17,400kg) | 8,488lb (3,850kg) | 7 + 10 pass-engers | 34mph (54.72km/h) | 1,243 miles (2,000km) | not available |
| d | one airship: LZ6A | August 1910 | 2 x 115-hp (85.7-kW) Daimler J4L petrol engines; 1 x 140-hp (104-kW) Maybach A-Z petrol engine | 565,030ft³ (16,000m³) of hydrogen in 18 gas cells | 472ft 5⅛in (144m) | 42ft 8in (13m) | not available | 41,005lb (18,600kg) | 9,634lb (4,370kg) | 7 + 10 pass-engers | 34mph (54.72km/h) | 1,243 miles (2,000km) | not available |
| e | two airships: LZ7 Deutschland; LZ8 Ersatz Deutschland | 19 June 1910 | 3 x 120-hp (89.5-kW) Daimler J4F petrol engines | 681,570ft³ (19,300m³) of hydrogen in 18 gas cells | 472ft 5⅛in (148m) | 45ft 11¼in (14m) | 34,392lb (15,600kg) | 49,383lb (22,400kg) | 15,873lb (7,200kg) | 8 + 20 pass-engerss | 37.35mph (60.11km/h) | 994 miles (1,600km) | not available |
| f | three airships: LZ9 (army Ersatz ZII); LZ10 Schwaben; LZ12 (army ZIII) | 26 June 1911 | 3 x 145-hp (108-kW) Maybach A-Z petrol engines | 629,000ft³ (17,800m³) of hydrogen in 17 gas cells | 459ft 3¾in (140m) | 45ft 11¼in (14m) | 29,982lb (13,600kg) | 45,525lb (20,650kg) | 15,542lb (7,050kg) | 8 + 20 pass-engers | 46.97mph (75.59km/h) | 901 miles (1,450km) | 8,040ft (2,450m) |
| g | two airships: LZ11 Viktoria Luise; LZ13 Hansa | 14 February 1912 | 3 x 150-hp (122-kW) Maybach B-Y petrol engines | 660,380ft³ (18,700m³) of hydrogen in 18 gas cells | 472ft 5⅛in (148m) | 45ft 11¼in (14m) | 33,400lb (15,150kg) | 47,840lb (21,700kg) | 14,440lb (6,550kg) | 8 + 25 pass-engers | 46.97mph (75.59km/h) | 684 miles (1,100km) | not available |

| Class | Number & designations | First flight | Powerplant | Gas capacity | Length | Maximum diameter | Typical empty weight | Typical gross lift | Typical disposable load | Comp-lement | Speed | Range | Static ceiling |
|---|---|---|---|---|---|---|---|---|---|---|---|---|---|
| h | six airships: LZ14 (navy L1); LZ15 (army Ersatz ZI); LZ16 (army ZIV); LZ17 Sachsen; LZ19 (army Desatz ZI); LZ20 (army ZV) | 7 October 1912 | 3 x 180-hp (134-kW) Maybach B-Y petrol engines | 803,050ft³ (22,740m³) of hydrogen in 18 gas cells (except LZ15, LZ16, LZ17, LZ19, LZ120 with 688,630ft³ [19,500m³] of hydrogen in 16 gas cells) | 518ft 4½in (158m) (except LZ15 and LZ16 at 465ft 10½in [142m] and LZ17, LZ19 and LZ120 at 459ft 3¾in [140m]) | 48ft 10½in (14.9m) | 39,462lb (17,900kg) for LZ14 | 57,540lb (26,100kg) for LZ14 and 50,044lb (22,700kg) for LZ16 | 18,078lb (8,200kg) for LZ14 and 10,585lb (4,800kg) for LZ16 | 20 | 47.42mph (76.31km/h) | 1,429 miles (2,300km) | not available |
| i | one airship: LZ18 (navy L2) | 9 September 1913 | 4 x 180-hp (134-kW) Maybach C-X petrol engines | 953,490ft³ (27,000m³) of hydrogen in 18 gas cells | 518ft 4½in (158m) | 54ft 5½in (16.6m) | 44,643lb (20,250kg) | 69,114lb (31,350kg) | 24,471lb (11,100kg) | 23 | 46.9mph (75.48km/h) | 1,305 miles (2,100km) | not available |
| k | one airship: LZ21 (army ZVI) | 10 October 1913 | 3 x 180-hp (134-kW) Maybach C-X petrol engines | 737,015ft³ (20,870m³) of hydrogen in 17 gas cells | 485ft 6⅝in (148m) | 48ft 10½in (14.9m) | 34,061lb (15,450kg) | 53,461lb (24,250kg) | 21,605lb (9,800kg) | 18 | 45.85mph (77.01km/h) | 1,181 miles (1,900km) | not available |
| l | two airships: LZ22 (army ZVII); LZ23 (army ZVIII) | 10 November 1913 | 3 x 180-hp (134-kW) Maybach C-X petrol engines | 781,860ft³ (22,140m³) of hydrogen in 18 gas cells | 511ft 9¾in (156m) | 48ft 10½in (14.9m) | 37,147lb (16,850kg) | 56,658lb (25,700kg) | 19,511lb (8,850kg) | 18 | 44.73mph (71.98km/h) | 1,181 miles (1,900km) | not available |
| m and m2 | 12 airships: LZ 24 (navy L3); LZ25 | 11 May 1914 | 3 x 180-hp (134-kW) Maybach C-X petrol engines | 793,515ft³ (22,470m³) of hydrogen in 18 gas cells | 518ft 4½in (158m) | 48ft 10½in (14.9m) | 37,257lb (16,900kg) | 57,540lb (26,100kg) | 20,282lb (9,200kg) | 16 | 52.34mph (84.23km/h) | 1,367 miles (2,200km) | 9,185ft (2,800m) |

(army ZIX); LZ27 (navy L4); LZ28 (navy L5); LZ29 (army ZX); LZ30 (army ZXI); LZ31 (navy L6); LZ32 (navy L7); LZ33 (navy L8); LZ34 (army LZ34); LZ35 (army LZ35); LZ37 (army LZ37)

| Class | Number & designations | First flight | Powerplant | Gas capacity | Length | Maximum diameter | Typical empty weight | Typical gross lift | Typical disposable load | Comp-lement | Speed | Range | Static ceiling |
|---|---|---|---|---|---|---|---|---|---|---|---|---|---|
| n | one airship: LZ26 (army ZXII) | 14 December 1914 | 3 x 180-hp (134-kW) Maybach C-X petrol engines | 882,860ft³ (25,000m³) of hydrogen in 18 gas cells | 528ft 10½in (161m) | 52ft 6in (16m) | 37,037lb (16,800kg) | 63,933lb (29,000kg) | 26,896lb (12,200kg) | 18 | 50.33mph (81km/h) | 2,051 miles (3,300km) | not available |
| o | two airships: LZ36 (army LZ36); LZ39 (army LZ39) | 8 March 1915 | 3 x 180-hp (134-kW) Maybach C-X petrol engines | 879,330ft³ (24,900m³) of hydrogen in 18 gas cells | 529ft 6½in (161.4m) | 52ft 6in (16m) | 39,241lb (17,800kg) | 63,713lb (28,900kg) | 24,471lb (11,100kg) | 16 | 52.79mph (85.24km/h) | 2,051 miles (3,300km) | not available |
| p | 22 airships: LZ38 (army LZ38); LZ40 (navy L10); LZ41 (navy L11); LZ42 (army LZ72); LZ43 navy L12); | 3 April 1915 | 4 x 210-hp (157-kW) Maybach C-X petrol engines | 1,126,530ft³ (31,900m³) of hydrogen in 15 gas cells (except in LZ44, LZ45 | 536ft 5in (163.5m) | 61ft 4¼in (18.7m) | 45,855lb (20,800kg) | 81,570lb (37,000kg) | 35,714lb (16,200kg) | 18 | 59.72mph (96.11km/h) | 2,672 miles (4,300km) | 9,185ft (2,800m) |

with a capacity of 1,115,935ft³ [31,600m³] of hydrogen in 18 gas cells; LZ51, LZ56, LZ57, LZ58, LZ60, LZ63 – all converted to LZ51A, LZ56A, LZ57A, LZ58A, LZ60A, LZ63A standard – with a capacity of 1,264,260ft³ [35,800m³] of hydrogen in 18 gas cells)

LZ44 (army LZ74); LZ45 (navy L13); LZ46 (navy L14); LZ47 (army LZ77);
LZ48 (navy L15); LZ49 (army LZ79); LZ50 (navy L16); LZ51 (army LZ81); LZ52 (navy L18); LZ53 (navy L17); LZ54 (navy L19); LZ55 (army LZ85);
LZ56 (army LZ86); LZ57 (army LZ57); LZ58 (army LZ88); LZ60 (army LZ90); LZ63 (army LZ93)

| Class | Number & designations | First flight | Powerplant | Gas capacity | Length | Maximum diameter | Typical empty weight | Typical gross lift | Typical disposable load | Comp-lement | Speed | Range | Static ceiling |
|---|---|---|---|---|---|---|---|---|---|---|---|---|---|
| q | 12 airships: LZ59 (navy L20); LZ61 (navy L21); LZ64 | 21 December 1915 | 4 x 240-hp (179-kW) Maybach H-S-Lu petrol engines | 1,264,260ft³ (35,800m³) of hydrogen in 18 gas cells | 585ft 7½in (178.5m) | 61ft 4¼in (18.7m) | 52,138lb (23,650kg) | 91,601lb (41,550kg) | 39,462lb (17,900kg) | 16 | 59.27mph (95.38km/h) | 2,672 miles (4,300km) | not available |
| | (navy L22); LZ65 (army LZ95); LZ66 (navy L23); LZ67 (army LZ97); LZ68 (army LZ98); LZ69 (navy L24); LZ71 (army LZ101); LZ73 (army LZ103); LZ77 (army LZ107); LZ81 (army LZ111) | | | | | | | | | | | | |
| r | 17 airships: LZ62 (navy L30); LZ72 (navy L31); LZ74 (navy L32); LZ75 (navy L37); LZ76 (navy L33); LZ78 | 28 May 1915 | 6 x 240-hp (179-kW) Maybach H-S-Lu petrol engines | 1,949,360ft³ (55,200m³) of hydrogen in 19 gas cells (except LZ62 with 1,942,295ft³ [55000m³] of hydrogen in 19 gas cells) | 649ft 7¼in (198m) | 78ft 5in (23.9m) | 69,224lb (31,400kg) | 140,653lb (63,800kg) | 71,429lb (32,400kg) | 17 | 50.1mph (80.63km/h) | 4,598 miles (7,400km) | 12,795ft (3,900m) |
| | (navy L34); LZ79 (navy L41); LZ80 (navy L35); LZ82 (navy L36); LZ83 (army LZ113); LZ84 (navy L38); LZ85 (navy L45); LZ86 (navy L39); LZ87 (navy L47); LZ88 (navy L40); LZ89 (navy L50); LZ90 (army LZ120) | | | | | | | | | | | | |
| s | two airships: LZ91 (navy 42); LZ92 (navy L43) | 22 February 1917 | 5 x 240-hp (179-kW) Maybach H-S-Lu petrol engines | 1,959,955ft³ (55,500m³) of hydrogen in 18 gas cells | 644ft 8¼in (196.5m) | 78ft 5in (23.9m) | 61,949lb (28,100kg) | 142,196lb (64,500kg) | 80,247lb (36,400kg) | 23 | 61.96mph (99.71km/h) | 6,462 miles (10,400km) | 16,405ft (5,000m) |
| t | two airships: LZ93 (navy L44); LZ94 (navy L46) | 1 April 1917 | 5 x 240-hp (179-kW) Maybach H-S-Lu petrol engines | 1,970,550ft³ (55,800m³) of hydrogen in 18 gas cells | 644ft 8¼in (196.5m) | 78ft 5in (3.9m) | 59,303lb (26,900kg) | 142,747lb (64,750kg) | 83,444lb (37,850kg) | 23 | 64.64mph (104.03km/h) | 7,146 miles (11,500km) | 17,060ft (5,200m) |
| u | five airships: LZ95 (navy L48); LZ96 (navy L49); LZ97 (navy L51); LZ98 (navy L52); LZ99 (navy L54) | 22 May 1917 | 5 x 240-hp (179-kW) Maybach H-S-Lu petrol engines | 1,970,550ft³ (55800m³) of hydrogen in 18 gas cells | 644ft 8¼in (196.5m) | 78ft 5in (23.9m) | 56,768lb (25,750kg) | 142,747lb (64,750kg) | 85,979lb (39,000kg) | 19 | 71.13mph (114.47km/h) | not available | 18,045ft (5,500m) |
| v | ten airships: LZ100 (navy L53); LZ101 (navy L55); LZ103 (navy L56); LZ105 (navy L58); LZ106 (navy L61); LZ107 (navy L62); LZ108 (navy L60); LZ109 (navy L64); LZ110 (navy L63); LZ111 (navy L65) | 8 July 1917 | 5 x 240-hp (179-kW) Maybach H-S-Lu petrol engines in LZ100 to LZ103; 5 x 245-hp (183-kW) Maybach Mb.IVa petrol engines in LZ105 to LZ111 (a standard to which LZ100 and LZ103 were later re-engined) | 1,977,610ft³ (56,000m³) of hydrogen in 14 gas cells | 644ft 8¼in (196.5m) | 78ft 5in (23.9m) | 55,115lb (25,000kg) | 143,298lb (65,000kg) | 88,183lb (40,000kg) | 19 | 66.88mph (107.63 km/h) with H-S-Lu engines and 71.13mph (114.47km/h) with Mb.IVa engines | 8,389 miles (13,500km) | 21,325ft (6,500m) |

| Class | Number & designations | First flight | Powerplant | Gas capacity | Length | Maximum diameter | Typical empty weight | Typical gross lift | Typical disposable load | Comp-lement | Speed | Range | Static ceiling |
|---|---|---|---|---|---|---|---|---|---|---|---|---|---|
| w | two airships: LZ102 (navy LZ57); LZ104 (navy L59) | 29 September 1917 | 5 x 240-hp (179-kW) Maybach H-S-Lu petrol engines | 2,419,040ft³ (68,500m³) of hydrogen in 16 gas cells | 743ft 3⅜in (226.5m) | 78ft 5in (9m) | 60,406lb (27,400kg) | 175,265lb (79,500kg) | 47,840lb (21,700kg) | 22 | 63.97mph (102.95km/h) | 9,942miles (16,000km) | 21,655ft (6,600m) |
| x | three airships: LZ112 (navy L70); LZ113 (navy LZ71); LZ114 (navy L72) | 1 July 1918 | 7 (later reduced to 6) x 240-hp (179-kW) Maybach Mb.IVa petrol engines | 2,196,560ft³ (62,200m³) of hydrogen in 15 gas cells (except LZ113A [upgraded LZ113] and LZ114 with 2,419,040ft³ [68,500m³] of hydrogen in 16 gas cells) | 692ft 7in (211.1m) except LZ113A (upgraded LZ113) and LZ114 at 743ft 1⅛in (226.5m) | 78ft 5in (23.9m) | 54,453lb (24,700kg) | 159,171lb (72,200kg) except LZ113A (upgraded LZ113) and LZ114 with 175,176lb (79,460kg) | 104,718lb (47,500kg) except LZ113A (upgraded LZ113) and LZ114 with 120,723lb (54,760kg) | 30 | 81.42mph (131.03 km/h) | 7,457 miles (12,000km) | 20,340ft (6,200m) |
| y | one airship: LZ120 Bodensee | 20 August 1919 | 4 x 245-hp (183-kW) Maybach mb.IVa petrol engines | 706,290ft³ (20,000m³) of hydrogen in 12 gas cells later increased to 796,340ft³ (22,550m³) of hydrogen in 13 gas cells | 396ft 4in (120.8m) later increased to 39ft 8⅔in (130.8m) | 61ft 4¼in (18.7m) | 29,101lb (13,200kg) | 51,367lb (23,300kg) | 22,046lb (10,000kg) | 16 + 21 pass-engers | 82.3mph (132.45 km/h) | 1,056 miles (1,700km) | 6,235ft (1,900m) |
| ZR-3 | one airship: LZ126 (USS Los Angeles) | 27 August 1924 | 5 x 400-hp (298-kW) Maybach VL-1 petrol engines | 2,472,015ft³ (70,000m³) of hydrogen (later helium) in 13 gas cells | 656ft 2in (200m) | 104ft 8in (31.9m) | 93,034lb (42,200kg) | 179,233lb (81,300kg) with hydrogen and 166,667lb (75,600kg) with helium | 86,199lb (39,100kg) | 28 + 20 pass-engers | 73.14mph (117.7km/h) | 7,767 miles (12,500km) | not available |
| | one airship: LZ127 Graf Zeppelin | 18 September 1928 | 5 x 530-hp (395-kW) Maybach VL-2 petrol engines | 2,648,585ft³ (75,000m³) of hydrogen and 1,059,435ft³ (30,000m³) of Blaugas in 16 gas cells | 776ft 3in (236.6m) | 100ft (30.5m) | 147,928lb (67,100kg) | 191,799lb (87,000kg) | 43,871lb (19,900kg) | 36 + 20 pass-engers | 79.6mph (128.1km/h) | 6,214 miles (10,000km) | not available |
| ZRS-4 | two airships: USS Akron; USS Macon | 25 September 1931 | 8 x 570-hp (425-kW) Maybach VL-2 petrol engines | 6,850,000ft³ (193,970m³) of helium in 12 gas cells | 785ft (239.3m) | 132ft 11in (40.5m) | 244,713lb (111,000kg) | 461,207lb (209,200kg) | 216,490lb (98,200kg) | 60 | 84mph (135.18km/h) | 6,835 miles (11,000km) | not available |
| | two airships: LZ129 Hindenburg; LZ130 Graf Zeppelin II | 4 April 1936 | 4 x 1,050-hp (783-kW) Daimler-Benz 602 diesel engines | 7,062,895ft³ (200,000m³) of hydrogen in 16 gas cells | 803ft 9⅔in (245m) | 135ft 2in (41.2m) | 286,596lb (130,000kg) | 511,464lb (232,000kg) | 143,298lb (65,000kg) | 40 + 50 (later increased to 72) pass-engers | 83.88mph (134.98km/h) | 10,253 miles (16,500km) | not available |

# Index

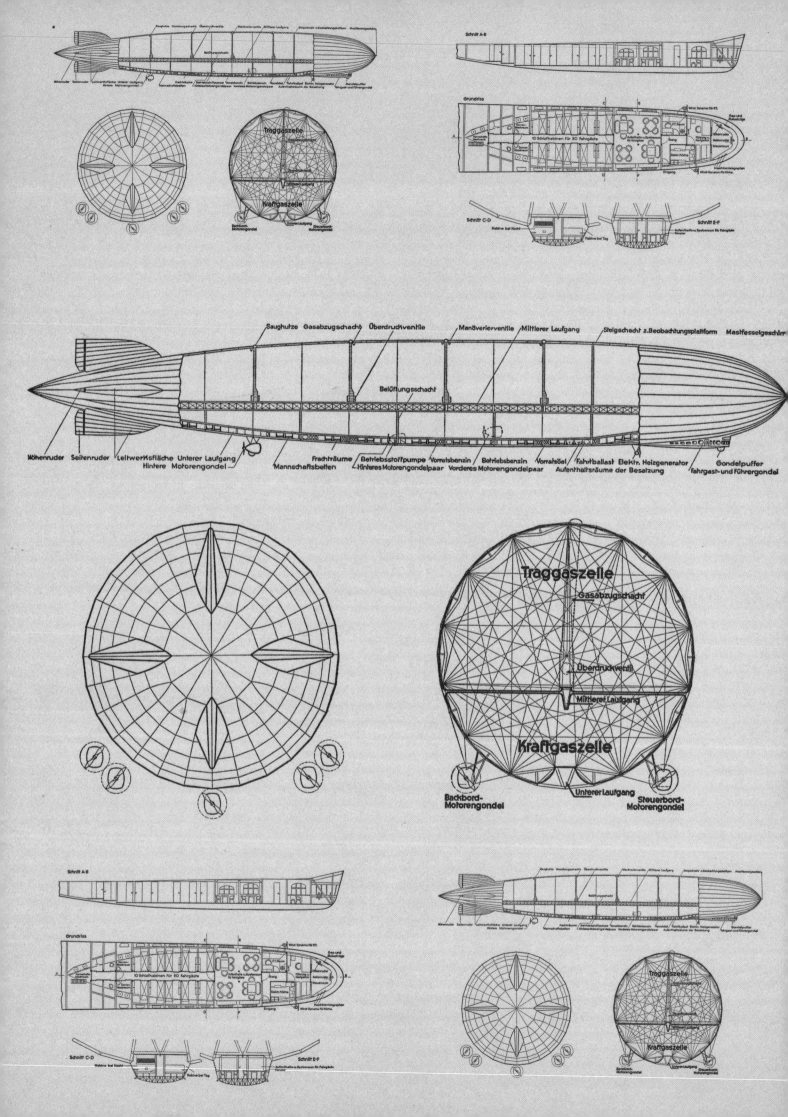

Saughutze  Gasabzugschacht  Überdruckventile  Manöverierventile  Mittlerer Laufgang  Steigschacht z.Beobachtungsplattform  Mastfesselgeschirr

Belüftungsschacht

Höhenruder  Seitenruder  LeitwerKsfläche  Unterer Laufgang  Frachträume  Betriebsstoffpumpe  Vorratsbenzin  Betriebsbenzin  Vorratsöel  Fahrtballast  Elektr. Heizgenerator  Gondelpuffer
Hintere Motorengondel  Mannschaftsbetten  Hinteres Motorengondelpaar  Vorderes Motorengondelpaar  Aufenthaltsräume der Besatzung  fahrgast- und Führergondel

Traggaszelle

Gasabzugschacht

Überdruckventil

Mittlerer Laufgang

Kraftgaszelle

Backbord-Motorengondel  Unterer Laufgang  Steuerbord-Motorengondel

Schnitt A-B

Grundriss

10 Schlafkabinen für 20 Fahrgäste

Wind Dynamo für RT.  Gas-und Ballastfüge

Eingang

Schnitt C-D

Kabine bei Nacht  Kabine bei Tag

Schnitt E-F

Aufenthalts-u.Speiseraum für Fahrgäste Fenster